TEN-MINUTE PLAYS: VOLUME 4

from

Edited by
Michael Bigelow Dixon and Liz Engelman
With a Foreword by **Jon Jory**

And an Article about
Teaching the Ten-Minute Play

IMPORTANT BILLING AND CREDIT REQUIREMENTS

All producers of any play in this volume *must* give credit to the Author of the Play in all programs distributed in connection with performances of the Play and in all instances in which the title of the Play appears for purposes of advertising, publicizing or otherwise exploiting the Play and/or a production. The name of the Author *must* also appear on a separate line, on which no other name appears, immediately following the title, and *must* appear in size of type not less than fifty percent the size of the title type.

FOREWORD

I've been interested in the gradual acceptance of the Polaroid picture as an art form. There is the sense somehow that is has less to do with artifice, that it is, so to speak, photography delivered raw and unvarnished. It has limitations of color and control but these very limitations give it a singular and fascinating tone. Well, this isn't too different, is it, from the short, short play. Would we say a play is less complex because it lasted ten minutes? Is a Zen loan or a haiku "less complex" than a narrative poem? It brings us to the matter of distillation, of boiling something down to its essence and thus giving it power and energy through reduction. The best of these plays are irreducible. They don't circle around the point, they are the point. They almost feel hot to the touch.

For the actor it means the pleasure of playing moments that have been built to, moments that are the result of a long process, moments the character has to go through, experience in order to get on with the rest of their life. We may not have seen or heard the preparation but the moments are inevitable and central. In that sense ten-minute plays are always fulcrums of change for the characters. They won't ever be the same after these ten minutes, whether for good or evil.

Yes, things happen fast in this form (which makes for absorbing theatre), but that's because characters are usually coiled springs of one kind or another. The wonderful thing about a ten-minute play is that is usually blows up in your face.

Oh, and metaphor. Because of their brevity they tend to be metaphor instead of simply containing metaphor. Thus, like the Polaroid picture they seem to transcend their limitations by admitting them. They are rough and ready and explosive and then they are gone. Like fireworks. And we can always use fireworks in the theatre, right?

Jon Jory
Producing Director
Actors Theatre of Louisville

QUICK STUDIES:
Teaching the First College Course on the Ten-Minute Play

In Fall 1996, I taught a college course based on a collection of plays from the National Ten-Minute Play Contest. The weekly, one hours seminar was designed for right-out-of-high school college freshmen. Most knew only a little about drama or theatre. Few knew very much about college. None of them knew a thing about ten-minute plays or that even such a thing existed.

Like ten-minute plays, freshman seminars stand in unapologetic defiance of venerated tradition. Academic seminars evolved in European universities as intimate gatherings of highly advanced students, all with extensive preparation and career ambitions in the same field. Seminars for freshmen—a relatively recent, oxymoronic American invention—place randomly selected, inexperienced students in a forum designed for advanced specialists. As a nose-thumbing iconoclast and pedagogical "work-in-progress," the freshman seminar is a kindred spirit to the ten-minute play and a natural format for the first college course devoted specifically to this genre.

I began the course with Jane Anderson's *Lynette at 3 A.M.**, principally because it contains many elements that appeal to college-age readers: humor, sound effects, a ghost with "attitude," bilingualism, sex talk, and homicide—something to accommodate virtually every taste. The decision was a fortunate one.

The students were initially drawn in by the play's "schtick," but quickly found themselves—quite naturally and with surprisingly little prodding from me—delving into its dramatic heart. As we read through and "staged" the play, the students quickly realized that the simple act of Lynette standing between her sleeping husband (whose emotional exhaustion has rendered him more dead than alive) and the passionate, newly-murdered Esteban (whose die-for-love sensuality makes him more alive than dead) creates a visual metaphor for the conflicts in her life and literally sets the stage for poignant self-discovery.

The students also realized that just a few sound effects and simple stage directions on a page can instantaneously create a highly textured emotional universe in which "impossible" characters and situations immediately become plausible... then powerful... then meaningful. And then they're gone.

Lynette became the measure by which subsequent works

were judged. We all became stopwatch Aristotles, using this ten-minute *Oedipus* to devise theories on why some plays succeed and others fail. Pairs of characters (not necessarily "couples") at a point of crisis became the preferred subject matter, with comprehensible resolution and closure highly recommended. (John Bishop's *Arizona Anniversaries** and Jason Katim's *The Man who Couldn't Dance** became class favorites, as did 1997 Festival winner *Misreadings*** by Neena Beber.)

Plays with strong social or political themes were viewed with less interest even if the students were sympathetic to the author's position. So were plays with more than four characters ("I can't handle the math," complained one student). And there *has* to be humor. As another student observed, "The phrase 'Ten-Minute Play' is funny. How can someone even think of writing one that isn't?"

A graduate school advisor once said to me, "A good course gets you interested in the subject. A great course screws up your life." The first college course on the ten-minute play may fit somewhere in between. While none of my students has dropped out of college to join a repertory company, three are now writing plays for next year's National Ten-Minute Play Competition. Two more have already begun organizing, eleven months in advance, a student safari to the 1998 Humana Festival of New American Plays in Louisville. And one student has eagerly agreed to be my uncompensated teaching assistant next fall when I offer the ten-minute play seminar to a new group of freshmen. To my way of thinking, that's a sufficient number of "screwed up" people to deem the course of unqualified success.

Dr. Thomas Greenfield
Dean of the College
SUNY Geneseo
Geneseo, NY

*originally published in *More Ten-Minute Plays from Actors Theatre of Louisville* by Samuel French, Inc.

**published in *Ten-Minute Plays: Volume 4 from Actors Theatre of Louisville,* by Samuel French, Inc.

TABLE OF CONTENTS

by

FREDERICK BAILEY

KEEPER
by Frederick Bailey
Directed by **Jonathan Summey**
Dramaturg: **Jenny Sandman**

Mitsuko ....Kimberly Gainer
Wilkinson .... James Edward Quinn
Stradling ....Brian Carter

PRODUCTION STAFF

Scenic Designer **Tom Burch**
Costume Designer **Justyn Jaymes**
Lighting Designer **Laura Wickman**
Sound Designers **Josh T. Wirtz**
Properties Designer **Mark Walston**
Stage Manager **Charles M. Turner, III**
Assistant Stage Managers **Anna Drum, Heather Fields,**
Daniel William Gregg

THE PLACE

The lobby of an off-off-Broadway-type waiver theatre in Los Angeles. The entrance from the outside is on stage right—there's a park-
ing lot out there. The box office, just inside the door, is not much
more than a high desk behind a railing, with a telephone. A side table
for refreshments sits at up center, with a 40-cup coffee urn, sugar,
creamer, honey, mustard, ketchup, salt and pepper. A digital clock
over the box office reads just after 7:00 pm. Posters from previous
productions adorn the walls. The entrance to the theatre itself is a set
of double doors up a corridor at up left. A person could stand in the
corridor and not be seen from the box office.

THE TIME

Tomorrow night.

KEEPER

(MITSUKO, a Japanese American woman in her 30s, enters down the corridor carrying a cash box and a reservation book. She's dressed in a nice-looking skirt and blouse and high heels. She's going to be taking care of the box office tonight. She empties a lobby ashtray into a wastebasket as she circles behind the high desk. She starts arranging her book and box. The telephone rings.)

MITSUKO. *(On the phone.)* Catapult Theatreworks, this is Mitzi... Hi, Charlie... Yeah... We got about 95 on the books for tonight. Four walk-ups and we're sold out... What *about* the coffee?... She's not?... But I'm running the box office tonight. I can't do both... All right, all right, I'll do it now. Okay? Just calm down. Nobody's here yet. I'm doing it right now. When are you getting here?... So I'm supposed to handle everything by myself until intermission? Thanks a bunch.

(MITSUKO hangs up, hurriedly plucks the box office cash out of the cash box, folds the wad of bills, puts it in her pocket, starts to pick up the coffee urn from the side table, when WILKINSON comes in through the front entrance.)

MITSUKO. Oh, you're early. We're not really open yet. The play doesn't start until eight. *(Something about the odd way he smiles at her makes her hesitate.)* You're here for the play, aren't you?
WILKINSON. Not exactly. I guess so. What's it called?
MITSUKO. "Tie Goes To The Runner."
WILKINSON. What's it about?
MITSUKO. I'm in kind of a rush. Have you got a reservation?
WILKINSON. No.
MITSUKO. Well, we've only got four seats left, so you'd better make up your mind.

WILKINSON. What's your name?
MITSUKO. Mitzi.
WILKINSON. Don't I know you from somewhere? You're a TV
star.
MITSUKO. I don't think so.
WILKINSON. You look like one.
MITSUKO. I'll be right back. Don't go away.
WILKINSON. I won't.

*(MITSUKO leaves in a hurry with the coffee urn. WILKINSON takes
out a notepad, makes notes, pacing the lobby, relaxed, unworried.
He hears a vehicle drive up outside, tires crunching on gravel. He
glances out the front door. He double-takes. He's shocked at what
he sees. He's rattled. He looks around, calms himself, trying to
figure out what he wants to do, what angle to play. He gets an
idea. He looks to see if Mitsuko is coming back. It would appear
she's not. He sits behind the box office desk, perching on a high
stool, as though he were the box office personnel. STRADLING
comes in the front entrance, looking around. He's pleased to see
he's the only other person here. STRADLING is an average guy in
his 30s, dressed in jeans and sports jacket for a night out.
WILKINSON is a slightly older guy in a good suit. He's easygoing
and charming.)*

STRADLING. Hi.
WILKINSON. Hello.
STRADLING. I have a reservation.
WILKINSON. That's good. What name?
STRADLING. Stradling.
WILKINSON. For one person? *(Is there a faint touch of derision
in WILKINSON's voice as he says that? STRADLING nods, vaguely
defensive, as he pulls out his wallet.)* One early bird...

(WILKINSON locates STRADLING's name in the book, checks it off.)

STRADLING. How much are the tickets?
WILKINSON. Ummm... *(He finds a flier for the production.)*
Twelve dollars. *(STRADLING gives him a twenty. WILKINSON*

*doesn't know the box office procedure, since he's playing it by ear.
He fumbles with the cash box, but there's nothing in it except stray
pieces of paper and a pencil. WILKINSON continues, referring to
the twenty.)* Got anything smaller?

STRADLING. *(Shakes his head.)* Sorry. *(WILKINSON pulls out
his own wallet and gives STRADLING his change. He puts the twenty
in the cash box.)* Thanks. You got a program?

*(WILKINSON looks, finds a stack of programs, hands one to
STRADLING.)*

WILKINSON. Enjoy the play.

STRADLING. I'm sure I will. Did that review in the *Times* hurt
your business any? *(WILKINSON shrugs noncommittally.)* Fuck the
Times, huh? It got a great review in the *Reader.*

*(STRADLING wanders off across the lobby, talking inaudibly to him-
self, generally happy and pleased, but still—there's something
gnawing at him around the edges. WILKINSON just sits in the
box office, eyeballing STRADLING but pretending not to.)*

STRADLING. Excuse me. Was there a guy in here, just before I
came in the door?

WILKINSON. A guy? No.

STRADLING. Maybe ten minutes ago?

WILKINSON. Nobody. You're the first one here.

STRADLING. You're sure about that?

WILKINSON. Uh-huh.

STRADLING. Absolutely sure?

WILKINSON. Yes.

STRADLING. Good. That's good.

*(STRADLING wanders aside. WILKINSON looks worried now, but
he covers it up.)*

WILKINSON. Why do you want to know?

STRADLING. Because that means I got here before he did.

WILKINSON. *(Gives him a blank look.)* Before who?

STRADLING. My keeper. See, it's always like this. I'm on my way here. Or wherever I'm going. I'm in the truck driving. *He* gets here first. Before me. He comes in, goes around to all the women in the lobby and tells them I never wash my genitals. Then he leaves. Two minutes later, I walk in, I don't know he's been here. I got no idea. And all the women look at me. "He doesn't wash his genitals. Yucchhhh." And I can't figure out why nobody wants to talk to me.

WILKINSON. Who's this guy?

STRADLING. Just some keeper. I don't know if it's a man. It could be a woman.

(WILKINSON chuckles as though amused at a whimsical children's story.)

WILKINSON. What does he or she look like?

STRADLING. How would I know? He's always gone before I arrive. I thought if I got here first tonight, he'd come in, he'd see me here, he'd split. Nobody would have this advance negative word on me. Maybe I could meet somebody. The part that really murders me is it's not true. I shower daily.

WILKINSON. I don't get it. Why would he or she do this?

STRADLING. It's an experiment. Probably a government experiment.

WILKINSON. *(Laughs.)* So you're a walking guinea pig. Don't you think that's a little... ?

STRADLING. A little what?

WILKINSON. I don't know.

STRADLING. Weird? Goofball?

WILKINSON. I wasn't going to say that. What kind of experiment?

STRADLING. "Individual effects of prolonged isolation in an ongoing social context." *(WILKINSON laughs indulgently, but underneath it he's really unnerved.)* Every once in a while he loses track of me. I get loose and I meet someone. And I wake up in the morning and she's there. Beside me. Oh man. I'm so relieved. For a few weeks I can wake up in the middle of the night and I'm not alone. But then somehow or other, I can't figure out how he does it. He finds me. And one day when I'm gone, he comes in and he tells the woman, "You don't know this guy, he's an asshole and a dumb shit," and then he fucks her and splits. I get home, and I say, "How are you, baby?" and she gets pissed off. She says, "You always ask me that." Couple of weeks later and she's gone. I can't figure out what happened. I'm sick of it.

WILKINSON. If you examine this, it doesn't make any real sense. If you've never seen the person, how do you know he exists? How do you know what he or she tells people about you if you're not there?

STRADLING. Things get back to me.

WILKINSON. It doesn't add up. You should talk to somebody about this.

STRADLING. You think I'm paranoid?

WILKINSON. Maybe you could use it as a stand-up routine in one of those open mike clubs, you know? One of those comedy places. You could develop it. I think it's good material.

(MITSUKO comes back through the double doors, carrying the coffee urn. It's heavy.)

STRADLING. Let me help you with that.
MITSUKO. Oh. Thanks.
STRADLING. Where's it going?
MITSUKO. On the table.

(They place it on the side table. STRADLING smiles at her. She smiles back, but then she notices WILKINSON sitting behind the desk. She gives him an odd look—she doesn't know what he's doing there. WILKINSON moves aside deferentially. Both STRADLING and WILKINSON watch her as MITSUKO gets down under the table and plugs the coffee urn into a socket. They exchange a silent look. She stands, dusting off her hands. She goes behind the desk.)

WILKINSON. Mr. Stradling's money is in the till. I gave him a program.

MITSUKO. *(Not sure how to react.)* You took his money?

WILKINSON. Uh-huh. I won't be watching the show tonight. Not if there's only four seats left.

(WILKINSON's implying he's seen it before, as if he were part of the staff. MITSUKO is puzzled, but WILKINSON has a certain charm.)

MITSUKO. Okay.

(MITSUKO takes the twenty out of the cash box, wondering what's going on with these two men, wondering if she should be worried. STRADLING stands perfectly still.)

WILKINSON. I gave him his change.
STRADLING. *(Stiffly, to WILKINSON.)* Where's the bathroom?

(WILKINSON points vaguely.)

MITSUKO. Through the doors, on the right.

(STRADLING nods, as though he's just had his suspicions confirmed. He goes off through the double doors. WILKINSON makes sure STRADLING has left. He turns back to MITSUKO in the box office, with his back to the double doors. STRADLING sneaks back out, crouching in the corridor where WILKINSON can't see him.)

WILKINSON. *(To MITSUKO.)* You know what that guy just said? *(He looks over his shoulder, but doesn't see STRADLING.)* He told me he never washes his genitals.
MITSUKO. *(Disgusted.)* Why not?
WILKINSON. Said he doesn't believe in it. Some kind of religious cult or something. Weird, huh?
STRADLING. *Liar!*

(STRADLING attacks WILKINSON. They struggle ferociously, knocking the coffee urn off the table, spilling water and coffee grounds. MITSUKO screams.)

MITSUKO. *Stop it! Stop it!*

(They fight. STRADLING forces WILKINSON down against the up center wall between the box office and the side table. STRADLING

pulls out a big knife. WILKINSON *screeches in terror. STRADLING plunges the knife into WILKINSON's belly. MITSUKO gasps in horror. WILKINSON is now frozen in shock. STRADLING slowly draws the blade out. He stabs WILKINSON with it two more times, fast, then jumps back into a fierce stance with a frightening howl. MITSUKO screams. She starts for the door. STRADLING moves lithely, interceding so she can't get out. But he doesn't touch her. He only smiles at her, hiding the knife behind his back. MITSUKO grabs the phone, punches 911. STRADLING calmly takes the phone out of her hand and hangs it up. He gives her a gentle smile. MITSUKO stares back at him, swallowing her terror. WILKINSON feels his stomach. He's not dead. He's not even wounded. He makes desperate gasping sounds, happy to be alive. STRADLING nods toward WILKINSON, indicating to MITSUKO that she should take a look. She realizes WILKINSON is unharmed.)*

MITSUKO. Are you all right? *(STRADLING takes the plastic ketchup dispenser off the side table and squirts ketchup all over WILKINSON. WILKINSON screws up his face. MITSUKO looks at STRADLING.)* What are you doing? Are you *nuts*?

(STRADLING demonstrates to both of them that it's a collapsible knife—the blade retracts into the handle. STRADLING shrugs.)
(WILKINSON scrambles up and rushes out the front door. STRADLING smiles at MITSUKO.)

STRADLING. Come on. I'll help you clean this up. You got a mop?
MITSUKO. I ought to call the cops.
STRADLING. Guy's been spreading lies about me. I had enough. I had to show him. What would you have done? *(He offers her the phone.)* My life is in your hands.

(MITSUKO takes the phone.)

MITSUKO. That's the most incredible line of bullshit I've ever heard.

(MITSUKO hangs up the phone.)

STRADLING. It's not a line. It's the truth.

MITSUKO. I believe you. *(She crosses away from him.)* It's still a line.

(She opens a narrow broom closet and takes out a bucket and mop.)

STRADLING. I guess anything a man says to a woman is a line. What's your name?

(She looks at him strangely. Long, motionless pause while she thinks about answering.)

MITSUKO. My name is Mitsuko.

(She tosses him the mop. He catches it. They smile at each other.)

THE END

MISREADINGS

by

NEENA BEBER

MISREADINGS
by
Neena Beber

Directed by **Jennifer Hubbard**

Presented by special arrangement with William Morris Agency, Inc.
Commissioned by Actors Theatre of Louisville

Ruth ....Maryann Urbano
Simone ....Jennifer London

Scenic Designer **Paul Owen**
Costume Designer **Kevin R. McLeod**
Lighting Designer **Ed McCarthy**
Sound Designer **Martin R. Desjardins**
Properties Designer **Ron Riall**
Stage Manager **Julie A. Richardson**
Assistant Stage Manager **Andrew Scheer**
Dramaturg **Liz Engelman**

MISREADINGS

(Lights up on SIMONE.)

SIMONE. It's important to dress right. I want to look slick. To look sleek. To look like a fresh thing. I've got a message. I'm the message. Study me, baby, because in ten minutes, I'm outta here.

(SIMONE lights a cigarette. Lights up on RUTH. A stack of blue exam composition books on her desk.)

RUTH. What are the issues for which you would kill? I like to ask my students this on their first day of class. I assign novels where the hero or heroine kills, or is killed. I try to bring it home. They tell me they would kill to defend their family. They'd kill to defend their friends. I ask them if they would kill for their country... for their freedom... what would it take?

SIMONE. I'd kill for a pair of Prada velvet platforms in deep plum. *Those* are to die for.

RUTH. Simone. I didn't know what she was doing in my class. Neither did she, apparently. *(To SIMONE.)* Nice segue, Simone; would we be willing to die for the same things we'd kill for? *(Out.)* She usually sat in the back, rarely spoke, wore too much lipstick and some costume straight out of, what, Vogue. When she did speak, it was always—disruptive.

SIMONE. I'd die for love except there ain't no Romeos, not that I've seen; I'd take a bullet for my daddy but he's already dead; I'd die of boredom if it were lethal, but I guess it isn't.

RUTH. If I couldn't inspire her, I wanted her gone. I'd asked her to come to my office hours. I asked her several times. She was failing, obviously. I would have let her drop the class, but it was too late

23

for that. She never bothered to come see me. Not until the day before the final exam. She wanted me to give her a passing grade. *(RUTH turns to SIMONE.)* How can I do that, Simone? You haven't even read the material. Have you read *any* of the material?

SIMONE. I don't find it relevant.

RUTH. If you haven't read it, how do you know? You may find yourself surprised. *Anna Karenina* is wonderful.

SIMONE. It's long.

RUTH. Why not give it a shot?

SIMONE. The books you assign are depressing. I don't want to be depressed. Why read stuff that brings you down? Kafka, Jesus Christ—I started it, okay? The guy was fucked up.

RUTH. So you were moved at least.

SIMONE. Moved to shut the book and find something more interesting to do.

RUTH. That's too bad; you might have found one of these books getting under your skin, if you stuck with it. Haven't you ever read something that's really moved you?

SIMONE. Nothing moves me, Dr. Ruth.

RUTH. I'm going to have to have to ask you to put out that cigarette.

SIMONE. Okay, ask. *(But she puts it out.)* See art or be art. I choose the latter.

RUTH. Somebody must be paying for this education of yours. I imagine they expect a certain return for their money.

SIMONE. How do you know I'm not the one paying for it?

RUTH. I don't believe someone who was spending their own money would waste it so flagrantly.

SIMONE. Okay, Dad chips in.

RUTH. Would that be the same father you said was dead?

SIMONE. That was a joke or a lie, take your pick.

RUTH. You're frustrating the hell out of me, Simone.

SIMONE. I don't consider it a waste, you know. I like the socialization part.

RUTH. If you fail out of this school, you won't be doing any more "socialization."

SIMONE. You assume that I'm failing the others.

RUTH. So it's just this class, then? That you have a problem with?

SIMONE. *(Referring to her grammar.)* Dangling. *(Beat.)* Do you enjoy being a teacher?

RUTH. Yes, I do.

SIMONE. So I'm paying for your enjoyment.

RUTH. It's not a sin to enjoy one's work, Simone.

SIMONE. I just don't think you should charge me, if it's more for your pleasure than for mine.

RUTH. I didn't say that.

SIMONE. Did you ever want to teach at a real school, not some second-rate institution like this?

RUTH. I like my job. You're not going to convince me otherwise.

SIMONE. Four-thousand two-hundred and ninety-eight.

RUTH. That is—?

SIMONE. Dollars. That's a lot of money. Do you think you're worth it? Do you think *this class* is *worth* it? Because I figured it out: this is a four credit class, I broke it down. Four-thousand two-hundred and ninety-eight. Big ones. Well, do you think that what you have to teach me is worth that? Come on, start talking and we'll amortize for each word.

RUTH. You're clearly a bright girl. You can't expect an education to be broken down into monetary terms.

SIMONE. You just did. That's a lot of money, right? It's, like, food for a starving family in a fifth-world country for a year at least. It's a car. Well, a used one, anyway. Minus the insurance. Suddenly this number doesn't sound so huge. It's a couple of Armani suits at most. I don't even like Armani. So hey, come on, can't you even say "Yes, Simone, I am worth two Armani suits. I have that to offer you..."

RUTH. I can't say that, no.

SIMONE. No useful skills to be had here.

RUTH. The money doesn't go into my pocket, by the way.

SIMONE. I think it should. It would be more direct that way; you'd feel more of a responsibility. To me. Personally. Don't you think, Dr. Ruth?

RUTH. I'd prefer that you not call me that.

SIMONE. Wrong kind of doctor, man. All you're interested in is a bunch of books written a hundred years ago, and the books written about those books; you're probably writing a book about a book written about a book right now, am I right?

RUTH. If you don't see the connection between books and life, you aren't reading very well. I want you to try. Can you do that? Books might even show you a way to live.

SIMONE. I'm already living, Dr. Ruth. Are you? Because it looks like you haven't changed your hair style in twenty-five years.

RUTH. You weren't even born then, Simone.

SIMONE. Stuck in your best year? Because I see you in a close-cropped, spiky thing.

RUTH. That's enough.

SIMONE. P. S.: You might want to do something about the way you dress.

RUTH. Have you been in therapy?

SIMONE. Don't think that's an original suggestion.

RUTH. I'm not suggesting anything. I simply want to point out that this is not therapy. I am a teacher, not your therapist. You can't just waltz into my office and say whatever hateful thing you please.

SIMONE. I don't know how to waltz.

RUTH. I'm giving up here, Simone. You don't like my class, you don't like me, you want to fail out, I can't stop you. *(RUTH goes back to her work. SIMONE doesn't budge.)* What?

SIMONE. Drew Barrymore would move me.

RUTH. Who?

SIMONE. I think Drew would do it. Getting to meet Drew.

RUTH. Who is Drew Barrymore?

SIMONE. Damn, you really should know these things. She's extremely famous. She's been famous since she was, like, born. I saw her on TV yesterday and she was so real. She connected. You know? You really might relate to your students better if you got a little more up to date.

RUTH. You might be right. But you might not be so behind in class if you spent a little less time watching television.

SIMONE. Drew is a *film* star, she's in *films*.

RUTH. You said you saw her on television.

SIMONE. Don't you even go to the movies? Probably only the ones that are totally L-Seven. And I know you don't know what that means. *(She makes an "L" and a "7" with her fingers.)* Square? Anyway, Drew was on TV because she was being interviewed. They have these daytime talk shows nowadays?

RUTH. I've heard of them.

SIMONE. And this chick was in the audience and she started to cry. Because she couldn't believe she was there in the same room with Drew, who's been famous forever, right? She was just, like, sitting there sobbing. And this chick, she had her bleached blond hair pasted down real flat, and she was wearing a rhinestone barrette just like Drew used to, but that whole look is so old Drew, so ten-minutes-ago Drew. The new Drew is sleek and sophisticated and coiffed and this girl, this girl who wanted to be Drew so bad, she wasn't even *current*.

RUTH. I don't think we're getting anywhere.

SIMONE. And that is so sad. Because the thing about Drew is, she's always changing. It's a constant thing with her, the change. And that is, like, what you've got to do... keep moving or you die. Drew knows that. How to invent yourself again and again so you can keep being someone that you like, the someone that you want to be. And once you're it, you've got to move on. Now where was it you were hoping we'd get to?

RUTH. The exam is tomorrow morning at 9AM. If you read the material, any of the material, I might actually be able to give you a passing grade. But right now I don't think we need to waste any more of each other's time.

SIMONE. *(Starts to go.)* You might have said that I go to the movies the way you read books. I would have pointed that out, Dr. Ruth.

RUTH. Well, I suspect we don't think very much alike.

(SIMONE turns back.)

SIMONE. A wall between our souls? *(RUTH looks at her, about to say something, about to reach out.)* I'm sorry if I've been rude. I'm sure a lot of people like your class. Maybe I wasn't raised well. I'm sure somebody's to blame.

(SIMONE goes.)

RUTH. The next day she showed up at nine on the dot. I felt a certain pride that I had somehow managed to reach her, that she was finally going to make a real effort, but she handed in her blue book after a matter of minutes. I was rather disgusted and let it sit there, until a pile formed on top of it, a pile of blue books filled with the scrawling, down-to-the-last-second pages of my other more eager, or at least more dutiful, students. Later I began to read them straight through from the top, in the order they were stacked in. I wasn't looking forward to Simone's.

In answering my essay question about how the novel *Anna Karenina* moves inevitably toward Anna's final tragic act, my students were, for the most part, thorough and precise. They cited all of the events that led to Anna's throwing herself in front of the train, touching on the many parallel plots and the broader social context. I was satisfied. I felt I had taught well this last semester. My students had learned.

In the blue book she had written, "All happy people resemble one another, but each unhappy person is unhappy in their own way." So I guess she had read *Anna K*; the opening sentence, at least. My first instinct was to correct the grammar of her little variation. There was nothing else on the page. I flipped through the book; she'd written one more line on the last page: "Any world that I'm welcome to is better than the one that I come from." I'm told it's a rock lyric. Something from the seventies. *Anna* was written in the seventies, too, funnily enough, a century earlier.

I would have given Simone an F, but I noticed she had already marked down the failing grade herself, on the back of the book. Or maybe the grade was for me.

By the time I came to it, days had passed. I didn't leap to conclusions. Come to think of it, Anna's suicide always takes me by surprise as well, though I've read the novel many times and can map its inexorable progression.

(SIMONE, just as before...)

SIMONE. That's a lot of money. Do you think you're worth it? Do you think *this class* is *worth* it?

(RUTH turns to her.)

RUTH. I live in worlds made by words. Worlds where the dead can speak, and conversations can be replayed, altered past the moment of regret, held over and over until they are bent into new possibilities.

(RUTH tries to reach out...)

SIMONE. Do you think I'm worth it? Am I? Am I? Am I?
RUTH. I live there, where death is as impermanent as an anesthesia, and the moment of obliteration is only... a black-out.

(SIMONE lights a cigarette as lights black out.)

SIMONE. Ten minutes, time's up—told you I'd be gone by now, baby.

(The flame illuminates her for a moment, darkness again.)

THE END

UNDER LUBIANKA SQUARE

by

CONSTANCE CONGDON

CAST LIST

Raya Tabachnikoff, age 40+, intelligent, well-educated, impoverished and desperate. Not Russian, from the Balkans.

Jennifer, age 25, a young, female American student from New Jersey. Nice, clueless. Heavy NJ accent.

Man, a mafia don, Russian-style.

PLACE

The metro station under Lubianka Square, near the Metropole Hotel, near theatrical Square, Moscow.

TIME

The present, 1997.

ACKNOWLEDGEMENTS

Thanks to Tanya Chebotarev, Michael Birtwistle, Cathy Ciepiela, and especially, Rebecca Teischman.

UNDER LUBIANKA SQUARE

(A 40+ year old woman runs into the space. She is dressed neatly but in out of style clothes, like from the seventies. She's carrying a beat-up gym bag with some inane slogan on it. This is RAYA. She's pursued by JENNIFER, an American student in her late twenties. JENNIFER is dressed stylishly casual, a little showily, in fact, and carries a camera bag. She speaks with a strong accent—New Jersey. RAYA has a Russian accent.)

RAYA. Are you crazy? Are you crazy?

JENNIFER. No.

RAYA. You act like a crazy person!

JENNIFER. *(Approaching her.)* I—

RAYA. Get away from me!

JENNIFER. Calm down. Someone—

RAYA. I hope. I hope they come arrest you.

JENNIFER. No! Stop it! Don't talk like that! Someone might *hear* you. Look—

RAYA. You are a bad person.

JENNIFER. I am not! I—I'm a student.

RAYA. Students can be bad. Students can be the worst.

JENNIFER. But I'm not. The worst. I'm just an American girl—woman.

RAYA. "Girl-woman"? What is that? Some TV talk from Los Angeles?

JENNIFER. You know Los Angeles?

RAYA. I'm not ignorant!

JENNIFER. I know that. I just wondered if you'd been there.

RAYA. I don't have money to travel.

33

JENNIFER. I'm sorry. Look, I'm sorry about everything. I'm sorry about the *whole fucking world*! I just wanted to take your picture. I mean, it was just a neat picture. You and all those women lined up, holding up those different jars and things—

RAYA. We are selling toiletries in the subway for money. That is "neat" to you.

JENNIFER. Well, *yeah*. I mean, it's social change and everything!

RAYA. What can you be thinking of—trying to take my picture! I am humiliated by what I have to do. You are the most rude American I have ever met.

JENNIFER. Canadian—I'm a Canadian.

RAYA. Say "house."

JENNIFER. *(American accent.)* House.

RAYA. Say "about."

JENNIFER. *(Faking a Canadian accent.)* Aboot.

RAYA. Too late. Why do you deny your country?

JENNIFER. I'm embarrassed about it. Particularly when people, like yourself, get mad at me for reasons I don't understand.

RAYA. You should get down on your knees and thank God every day you are an American.

JENNIFER. You sound like my father. Isn't that funny? He will be, like, so amazed to hear that some Russian woman—

RAYA. I am *not* Russian! I am from the Balkans!

JENNIFER. But this is *Russia*. Why be here... then?

(RAYA pauses to try to take in JENNIFER's complete lack of knowledge.)

RAYA. When history was taught to you, you were napping? Drawing pictures of Elvis on your notebook, perhaps?

JENNIFER. Elvis? Hardly. He was disgusting. Why people liked him, I don't know. He was fat.

RAYA. Nichevo. Nevermind. I'm going.

JENNIFER. Wait. I feel bad. Let me buy something. What's that?

RAYA. Hairspray.

JENNIFER. I'll buy that.

RAYA. Dollars.

JENNIFER. I have some Finmarks, some centimes, rubles—

RAYA. No rubles. No dollars? Finmarks, then.
JENNIFER. Wait. Here's a dollar.

(RAYA sees inside JENNIFER's purse.)

RAYA. What's that? Cigarettes?
JENNIFER. Merits.
RAYA. No L&Ms? Camels? Marlboro hard pack?
JENNIFER. Those will kill you. L&Ms? Who smokes L&Ms?
RAYA. My son.
JENNIFER. Okay. Here's a dollar.
RAYA. I need more.
JENNIFER. It's a little can of hairspray.
RAYA. Do you know how much this would cost you at GUM?
JENNIFER. What is "GUM"? Oh, that terrible mall.
RAYA. It is wonderful. Six years ago it smelled of urine and had no merchandise except some pathetic Russian-made goods.
JENNIFER. It still smells of urine.
RAYA. It does NOT! It has a BODY SHOP! You can buy French mousse for your hair—Yves Rouchet—excellent brands like that!
JENNIFER. All right. If you say so.
RAYA. You can buy anything in Moscow now!
JENNIFER. If that's so, why are you dressed like that?
RAYA. Because you silly, vapid American baby cow, I HAVE NO MONEY!! Why do you think I'm selling hair spray in the subway?!
JENNIFER. Your English is very good.
RAYA. So is my French, my German, and my Czech. Sprechen zie Deutsch? Parlez vous Français? *(In French.)* Peutêtre tu serais plus gentille si tu parles le français. (Perhaps you would be nicer if you spoke French.)
JENNIFER. I'm sorry. I only speak English.
RAYA. I must have three dollars for the hairspray. Unless you have some condoms.
JENNIFER. Wait. I have—

(JENNIFER digs in her purse, finds something.)

RAYA. This is—what is this?

JENNIFER. It's a condom. "In case of emergency, break plastic and save a life."

RAYA. It's a toy.

JENNIFER. It's a keychain. From GMHC. Gay Men's Health Crisis. Keep it.

RAYA. I don't need a keychain. I need a condom.

JENNIFER. HERE.

(JENNIFER hands her all her money of various kinds.)

RAYA. *(Hands JENNIFER the hair spray.)* Here.

JENNIFER. Wait.

RAYA. No exchanges. No refunds.

JENNIFER. WAIT! I can't use this.

RAYA. Why not?

JENNIFER. Fluorocarbons. It has fluorocarbons.

RAYA. And this is important? Why?

JENNIFER. Fluorocarbons are bad.

RAYA. Life is bad.

JENNIFER. No, I mean it. This stuff is very bad. I can't—I won't use it.

RAYA. Then SELL IT TO SOMEONE!

JENNIFER. Look—I have some standards! And the environment is one of them. This hair spray is evil.

RAYA. Look, Minnie Mouse, many things are evil. Stalin was evil. Hitler was evil, only not as evil as Stalin.

JENNIFER. Stalin was more evil than Hitler? Oh, I don't think so—

RAYA. You don't think? Twenty million people *dead*. Entire cultures—songs, history, language, people—*swept off the face of the earth* by his withered arm. People we never knew and never will know. So he is the tyrant of the Twentieth Century. Think of all the other centuries and the buried towns, destroyed down to their fragments. You pick up a rock with some marking on it, think it's Greek—maybe it's part of a story stone from some hill people who called themselves by a name we will never hear. Spoke a language we will never hear. Knew secrets we will never discover. That is evil. Hairspray is not evil.

JENNIFER. But there's a hole in the ozone.

RAYA. A what in the what?

JENNIFER. Above Antarctica. A big hole. They've photographed it.

RAYA. People are starving and your country is spending money taking pictures of a hole above a continent where no one could live???

JENNIFER. But it affects all of us! We need the ozone layer because it protects us from the UV rays of the sun.

RAYA. So fat ladies in Miami don't get skin cancer?

JENNIFER. How can you know so much and not know this important fact?

RAYA. What "fact"? What are you talking about? You are a child! The fact is I have an advanced degree in classical and Biblical literature from Moscow University. I was translating Biblical literature from the Greek just seven years ago. The fact is I am unemployed and have to take care of my husband who has heart pain every night. The fact is my grandchild is sickly and we have to make his baby food from bad ingredients because we can't buy good vegetables and meat. The facts are that seven of us are living in two rooms and we are educated, civilized people! With sensibility and pride and an unfortunately highly-developed inability to lie to ourselves! We wash out condoms so we can have sex without getting pregnant. Because we can't pay for birth control pills. And because I have already had eight abortions in my life and my daughter-in-law has had three and we still can conceive, in spite of all the scraping and damage. Now those are the facts!

JENNIFER. You know you just may be too hostile to sell anything to anyone. Have you thought about that? I mean, people don't like to be yelled at. In my opinion, there's too much yelling in the world. I turn on the TV and there are people yelling at each other and at the cameras and I ask, Jennifer, what are they all so angry about? I mean, everyone has problems! I, myself, have problems.

RAYA. What problems do you have?

JENNIFER. Well—thanks for asking—I, right now, have to pee and don't know where there's a bathroom. *And*, I'm not through, so don't give me that look. *And, I—*

(A large Russian MAN, in a slick-surfaced suit, very eurotrash/mafia don, enters and stares at RAYA. He is suave, warm and gracious to JENNIFER and threatening to RAYA.)

MAN. *(To JENNIFER.)* Priviet.

JENNIFER. "Private"? No, we're not private. I don't know her, actually—we just met—are you a... policeman?

(MAN laughs a lot at this.)

JENNIFER. What's so funny?

RAYA. He said "hello," that's all. "Priviet" means "hello."

JENNIFER. Wait. I can say a couple of things. *(To MAN.)* Do-bro Oo-tra.

MAN. *(Very gracious.)* Good evening—viecher. Dobry viecher, young lady.

JENNIFER. *(Titillated.)* Oh. Thanks. *(Sudden realization.)* Gosh, is it evening? I'm supposed to meet my friends at my hotel—I don't even know where I am.

MAN. Metropole Hotel is that way.

JENNIFER. Thanks. How did you know which hotel I was staying at.?

MAN. I had a lucky guess.

JENNIFER. Well, I should be going. *(Hands RAYA back the hairspray.)* Keep this. And the money.

MAN. *(To RAYA, in Russian.)* Ty opiat'u metro torguesh? I mne nichego ne otstiogiuaesh Plati, ato skvartiroi rasproshshaeshsia! (You were selling in the subway again? YOU BETTER PAY ME MY SHARE OR YOU WILL LOSE YOUR FLAT! Do you understand?)

JENNIFER. Do you know each other?

MAN. Yes, we're old friends.

JENNIFER. I figured as much. I though maybe you were her husband.

MAN. No. Her husband is a small man.

JENNIFER. With a heart condition.

MAN. Yes, he has a weak, weak heart. From too much worry. It's very bothersome—change. Change is very hard to live through. Many, many didn't live through it. And many more will not, also.

RAYA. *(About the eternality of mafia/KGB/thug power.)* We are married. Since time began. And we will never, never be separated, it seems.

JENNIFER. Oh, then you are married. I thought you said he was sick, your husband. *(To MAN.)* You don't look sick. You look really, really healthy.

MAN. Thank you for the compliment. I try to keep in shape. I eat well. I eat very well, in fact. For lunch, I had a chimichanga a La Kantina on Tverskaya Street. It cost twelve American dollars. It had meat, lots of it, cheese, pouring out of it. And five small tomatoes— fresh and good. Then I had apple pie, deep dish American apple pie with ice cream on it, for pudding. I mean, dessert. And I drank two glasses of milk. And a Coke.

RAYA. He is not my husband.

JENNIFER. But—

MAN. Raya means that we are married another way. Don't you, Mrs. Tabachnikoff?

RAYA. Yes.

JENNIFER. How? I don't understand.

RAYA. You should have stayed awake in history, detochka. It's already made your country and you can't see it.

JENNIFER. What? What are you two talking about? You're speaking English, but I can't understand what you're talking about!

RAYA. You will never grow up! You will lose your country because you refuse to grow up! Become educated!

JENNIFER. Why? It hasn't done you any good, has it? I mean, has it? You're selling shit in the subway. And yelling at tourists. You have no baby food! No heart medicine! No condoms! What has your education gotten you? History? I HATE FUCKING HISTORY! IT'S FUCKING BORING! IT HAS NOTHING TO DO WITH ME! WE STARTED OVER! DO YOU HEAR ME? WE STARTED OVER! WITH OUR OWN RULES!! I'M AN AMERICAN! AND I AM FINE! LOOK AT THESE CLOTHES! LOOK AT THIS HAIRCUT! THIS CAMERA BAG! I EAT WELL! I SLEEP WELL! *(JENNIFER begins pummeling RAYA with her camera bag.)* I'M GODDAM FUCKING HAPPY!!! HAPPY, DO YOU HEAR ME!!! HAPPY!!!!!

MAN. *(Getting JENNIFER off RAYA.)* Wait! Wait! Stop now! *(Taking camera bag.)* This is heavy.

JENNIFER. Oh god. I forgot that had my camera in it. Is it okay? Is she okay?

MAN. She's fine.

JENNIFER. Are—are you okay?
RAYA. I'm fine.
JENNIFER. I'm really sorry. I—I never do that! I swear!
RAYA. I'm fine.
JENNIFER. I've never hit anyone—ever... before.
RAYA. Perhaps you never had a good enough reason.
JENNIFER. I was brought up better than this.

(But to RAYA "this" means the subway and the way she has to live.)

RAYA. That is obvious.
JENNIFER. I'm a good person.
RAYA. So am I.

(JENNIFER gets some money from some place where she's hidden it—her bra or her shoe.)

JENNIFER. Here is all my money—that I'm carrying.
MAN. No, no, she doesn't need it. Her son will drink it up.
JENNIFER. I thought he only smoked.
RAYA. He does whatever he can.

(MAN folds the money back into JENNIFER's hand.)

MAN. Don't encourage her. Allow me to walk you to your hotel.
JENNIFER. Thank you. Spah-see-bah.
MAN. Pahzhaloostah, my dear.

(He starts to lead JENNIFER off, but JENNIFER is compelled to finish something with RAYA.)

JENNIFER. *(To RAYA.)* You know, we have people like you in America. Homeless people—lots of them—in the subways. But they're nicer to us. You know? They don't lecture us. They're not angry like you. Some of them are crazy and drunk and on drugs, but they mind their own business. Maybe they're not as smart as you, but they know how to treat people. You could learn something from them.

RAYA. I'm not homeless. I have a home.

MAN. Yes. Why don't you go there. *(Patronizing her.)* Detochka.

JENNIFER. I think she called *me* that. What does it mean?

MAN. My dear little child.

JENNIFER. *(To RAYA.)* Oh, you were being nice. I feel really bad now. It's just so hard to understand other people from other, you know, lands sometimes. *(Trying too hard to say it right.)* Dos Viy-dan-ya.

(JENNIFER leaves with the MAN.)

RAYA. *(To the audience.)* "And so I say unto you, the first shall become last and the last shall become first. And the merchants of the world shall weep over Babylon but all their fine goods will not save her. Behold, we come as thieves in the night and knock at your door. Blessed is he who is vigilant."

(RAYA exits.)

THE END

HEAD ON

by

ELIZABETH DEWBERRY

HEAD ON
by **Elizabeth Dewberry**
Directed by **Shirley Jo Finney**

CAST

Anne ....Adale O'Brien
Anne's Therapist ....Dee Pelletier

CHARACTERS

ANNE: A robust woman in her early sixties
ANNE'S THERAPIST: A slender, intelligent woman in her mid-forties

PLACE & TIME

Greenroom of the Oprah Winfrey Show. The present.

Commissioned by Actors Theatre of Louisville
Presented by special arrangement with Elaine Markson Agency

Scenic Designer **Paul Owen**
Costume Designer **Laura Patterson**
Lighting Designer **Brian Scott**
Sound Designer **Martin R. Desjardins**
Properties Master **Mark J. Bissonnette**
Dramaturg **Michael Bigelow Dixon**

HEAD ON

(The greenroom of the Oprah Winfrey show, ten minutes before tap-
ing. The therapist paces anxiously, looking at her watch. Anne
enters, in shock, and the therapist runs over to her.

THERAPIST. Oh, thank God you're here. *(Double take.)* Anne?
What are *you* doing here?

ANNE. I'm sorry I'm late. I saw a wreck.

THERAPIST. But you're not multiorgasmic.

ANNE. No. I'm fine.

THERAPIST. Oh God.

ANNE. I wasn't *in* the wreck. I just saw it happen. I was so afraid
I was going to be late. I've wanted to be on *Oprah Winfrey* forever,
it's my most recurrent fantasy, and now here I am.

THERAPIST. *Are* you?

ANNE. What?

THERAPIST. Multiorgasmic.

ANNE. I don't think so.

THERAPIST. Who told you to come here?

ANNE. Your receptionist. Do I look bad? I brought another outfit
if you don't like this one. This all happened so fast I didn't have time
to buy anything. If it hadn't been for the wreck...

THERAPIST. What did she tell you?

ANNE. You were going on Oprah to talk about your book and the
client you had coming on with you canceled and would I go on instead.

THERAPIST. Oh God.

ANNE. What? I know I just started seeing you, but you've already been a big help to me, dealing with Jerry's death. I have a lot to say.

THERAPIST. It has to be somebody who's multiorgasmic.

ANNE. Jerry had a bad heart.

THERAPIST. Were you ever multiorgasmic, even by yourself?

ANNE. I never had *one* orgasm. I can't say that on TV. I've never told anyone that before.

THERAPIST. We go on in eight minutes. I can't replace you.

ANNE. It's not my fault. There was a wreck, a head-on collision. But I can do this.

THERAPIST. I know it's not your fault.

ANNE. Two people died. Traffic's still backed up for miles.

THERAPIST. I'm not blaming you. I'm sorry.

ANNE. I'm an official witness, in the police reports. That takes time. Everybody was late to everywhere they were going. Have you ever witnessed a wreck?

THERAPIST. Yes. I have. Can we talk about this later? Right now...

ANNE. Of course. I'm sorry.

THERAPIST. I mean, there's nothing we can do about the wreck.

ANNE. Of course not.

THERAPIST. This was such a great opportunity, *Oprah Winfrey.* I could have been a best-seller. I had this client who was perfect, at age fifty-seven after three months of therapy with me she became multiorgasmic.

ANNE. Why isn't she here?

THERAPIST. She broke her hip.

ANNE. You can break your hip?

THERAPIST. No, she fell in the bathtub.

ANNE. That's too bad.

THERAPIST. It's not the same if you don't have somebody, a real person, to say it works.

ANNE. I'm sorry I haven't read your book, but tell me what to say, and I'll say it. What's the book about?

THERAPIST. Postmenopausal sex.

ANNE. I just wanted to meet Oprah Winfrey. I wanted to talk to her. Sometimes in my imagination I think of her as my daughter— not by Jerry, of course—and I just wanted to shake her hand. I thought maybe after the show we'd hug. Is that asking too much?

THERAPIST. No.

ANNE. I bid on a dress of hers once at a charity auction. Somebody else outbid me, though. I wanted to go twenty dollars higher but Jerry said it's a used dress, we can get you a new one for less than that. Then, of course, we didn't. That's how things went with him.

THERAPIST. And he never brought you to orgasm.

ANNE. Well, I don't know about that.

THERAPIST. Yes you do.

ANNE. I might have had one and forgotten.

THERAPIST. You wouldn't forget.

ANNE. I think sex is overrated anyway. I can't imagine writing a whole book about it. What did you say?

THERAPIST. Have you ever just wanted to ram yourself into something?

ANNE. You know I have. Maybe I could read a chapter real fast. If only that wreck hadn't happened. Look, I'm still trembling.

THERAPIST. You can't read it in six minutes.

ANNE. Right, so tell me. I once heard my mother say if feels like a sneeze between your legs. Should I say that?

THERAPIST., Why don't you focus on the spiritual dimension of sex? Two human beings coming together, each giving their body over to the other, moving out of themselves into the other...

ANNE. It sounds like a head-on collision. *(Beat.)* I'm sorry. I'm wrong.

THERAPIST. No, you're right. It does.

ANNE. Both drivers died. The debris was so bad the ambulances almost hit each other. *(Beat.)* What was the wreck you saw?

THERAPIST. My husband and his girlfriend.

ANNE. Oh.

THERAPIST. He was sitting in the car on a country road waiting for her and she plowed into him at sixty miles an hour.

ANNE. Did they die?

THERAPIST. No, they both had airbags.

ANNE. Those things are amazing. I wish I could go through life wearing airbags in my clothes. I don't think they had airbags this morning. I don't have them, my car doesn't.

THERAPIST. Right after she hit his car she jumped out of hers screaming, "You can't do this to me. I love you. I thought you loved me." Can you imagine?

ANNE. Amazing.

THERAPIST. I can still hear her saying that. I remember thinking that was what I wanted to yell at him, and she'd taken that too.

ANNE. *(Touching the doctor gingerly.)* I'm sorry.

(Short silence.)

THERAPIST. Five minutes. This is awful.

ANNE. Tell me something to say. I wish I'd read the book. I really ought to read more.

THERAPIST. It has exercises you can do with your partner.

ANNE. But Jerry's dead!

THERAPIST. Maybe you could do them with Oprah.

ANNE. Sex exercises?

THERAPIST. No, it's just ways of developing intimacy, touching each other's inner selves.

ANNE. I already know her inner self. I watch her every day. I know every outfit she owns. I wonder if she's ever going to sell any more of her dresses.

THERAPIST. Why do you want one?

ANNE. Because I want to know what it feels like to be her. Maybe I'll never know what it's like to be rich or famous, but I could know what it feels like to step into the dress of a woman who's beautiful, who knows how to talk to people and how to listen to them. I'd zip her zipper up my back and feel her sleeves on my arms and close my eyes and just for a minute, I'd let myself pretend I was not just in her dress, I was in *her* and I'd become her and she'd become me. I want to do that before I die. *(Short silence.)* I think they died instantly. They would've had to. They were completely smashed together. You couldn't tell one car from the other.

THERAPIST. I would imagine.

ANNE. Jerry took several days. He went into a coma. He had tubes hooking him up to every kind of machine there is. It was awful. And then the trial lasted for months.

THERAPIST. Can we try to put that off for an hour, talk about it as soon as the show is over? Would you do that for me?

ANNE. I'm sorry, you're right, I'm obsessing.

THERAPIST. That's not what I said.

ANNE. You actually saw your husband's wreck happen?

THERAPIST. I told you.

ANNE. My heart was pounding so hard and so fast I could feel it all the way through my body and my skin went tight and hot and I had to fight to keep my eyes open and it was coming and coming, I knew what was going to happen, I knew. And then it did and I felt the impact in my teeth and the whole world was crashing noises and echoes of crashing noises and spinning and then I heard my voice, my own voice above all the clatter, and I realized I'd been screaming and I stopped. *(Beat.)* Is that how it was for you?

THERAPIST. I was hiding behind a tree. I had a camera with me and I was going to take pictures of them having sex and then I was going to divorce him, and when I saw her car coming, I saw what she was going to do, and I hoped he'd die.

ANNE. You were lucky.

(THERAPIST looks at her in a question.)

ANNE. I think if Jerry's girlfriend had tried to kill him, even if she'd failed, I could have gotten what I needed from that. Then I wouldn't have had to do it myself.

(Pause while therapist looks at her watch.)

THERAPIST. We can't talk about this right now. In two minutes...

ANNE. I know, I'm sorry.

THERAPIST. Don't talk about Jerry on the show.

ANNE. I promise.

THERAPIST. Not a word.

ANNE. Nothing.

THERAPIST. He never existed. You're just beginning therapy...

ANNE. I had therapy in jail.

THERAPIST. No, you never went to jail. You're a widow beginning private therapy and you're a typical postmenopausal woman in the sense that you have deep longings for human connection inside you that you don't know how to address because you haven't read my book, and I'm going to tell you what you should do, and you're going to sit there and say I'm right, okay?

ANNE. Okay.

THERAPIST. And after the show, right after you hug Oprah, we'll get in our cars and go to my office and we'll have a long session.

ANNE. We'll get in our cars.

THERAPIST. And go to my office.

ANNE. I don't have airbags.

THERAPIST. It's time to go.

ANNE. Do I look okay?

THERAPIST. You look beautiful. Right now, you're wearing the dress of a beautiful woman.

ANNE. Jerry was killed in a car crash. I ran into him with my car in the yard before I hit the house.

THERAPIST. It's okay.

ANNE. I wasn't trying to kill him. I was just trying to get him to listen to me. Afterwards I got out of the car and my head was bleeding so bad I could hardly see but I made my way over the bricks to him and I held him in my arms, my blood dripping on his face, and I said, "When this is all over, can we talk?"

THERAPIST. You and I, we'll talk.

ANNE. What did you do after the girlfriend yelled at your husband?

THERAPIST. I took pictures of them. Then I told them to go fuck themselves and filed for divorce.

ANNE. You look beautiful, too.

THERAPIST. Come on.

ANNE. Do you have airbags?

THERAPIST. Yes.

THE END

COURTING PROMETHEUS

by

CHARLES FORBES

COURTING PROMETHEUS
by Charles Forbes
Directed by **Scot Anthony Robinson**
Dramaturg: **Liz Engelman**

Rita.................. ....Rachel Mattison
Lou ....Christopher R.C. Bosen

Scenic Designer **Tom Burch**
Costume Designer **Justyn Jaymes**
Lighting Designer **Laura Wickman**
Sound Designer **Elizabeth Rhodes**
Properties Designer **Mark Walston**
Stage Manager **Charles M. Turner, III**
Assistant Stage Managers **Anna Drum, Heather Fields,**
Daniel William Gregg

CHARACTERS

RITA, 28. A young professional. She is attractive in a reserved manner. Large glasses, hair pulled back.

LOU, 27. A young professional as well. Attractive, possibly a little overweight. Dark pants, bright tie.

SETTING

The modern office cubicle. Two desks directly face each other. A division wall separates the desks. With the exception of memos, pictures, etc. on the division wall, the cubicle is clean, bland and sterile.

COURTING PROMETHEUS

(*AT RISE: Sounds of phones and copiers and distant voices. RITA, head down in her paperwork, scribbles diligently. LOU, with hands in lap, stares at the division in front of him. They work for an extended amount of time. RITA quietly sneezes.*)

LOU. God bless you.

RITA. (*Without looking up.*) I don't believe in God and I don't believe in you. Leave me alone and let me work.

LOU. You don't believe in God or me?

RITA. I'm trying not to. Denial.

LOU. I can't speak for God, but "ouch." Look, I know... last night, a bit premature. Would you believe that I've admired you from afar, from over here, for months. Don't let the speed of...

RITA. Drop it. I've got to have the Rossman account balanced by five. I just want to forget about the whole thing.

LOU. I don't. I had a good time.

RITA. No you didn't, you got laid. There's a difference.

LOU. No, I had a good time *and* got laid.

(*RITA checks herself. She speaks in a voiced whisper, attempting to keep the conversation private. LOU speaks a little louder, but still aware of the office around him.*)

RITA. Look, I'm not blaming you. Don't think I'm going to blame you. The responsibility lies on my shoulders, my situation.

LOU. I had a good time. Why won't you believe me?

RITA. At my age, it is not logical for me to believe guys like you.

LOU. Logical? Age? Rita, you're twenty-eight.

RITA. Almost twenty-nine. And what's after that? Look, you don't have to let me down easy or feel like you have to take me out again. I'm not into stroking consciences right now.

LOU. Wanna grab a bite to eat when you finish? *(He looks at his watch.)* It's almost five.

RITA. Either you can't hear me over there or you really feel guilty. You're Catholic aren't you. Damn it.

LOU. No, I'm not and I don't! Feel guilty. Not really. Not unless you think I'm the type of guy who goes to office parties in hopes of scoring with his cubicle partner. I'm not. I don't feel guilty. But I'm not going to lie to you, Rita, I do feel something.

RITA. *(Irritated.)* Oh, do you? What you think you feel is an incredible pressure placed on your male psyche by every other one night stand you've ever had, no, no—placed on you by womanhood as a whole that tells you if you order the goods C.O.D., you have to pay for them when they show up, even if they are damaged!

LOU. *(Pauses.)* No. I'd like to go out with you.

RITA. You're not listening Lou. I can't afford to be with anyone right now. It has to be this way.

LOU. What? Loneliness?

RITA. Oh don't use romantic little words like "loneliness." That has nothing to do with it.

LOU. I didn't know there was romance in loneliness. You're lonely.

RITA. I am not! I'm... just... A constant dull ache is much more manageable than pangs of need. I am a person surrounded by manageable things Lou. You are not manageable.

LOU. I never hope to be. There is a big difference between being manageable and being...

RITA. Happy? Is that what you were going to say? You are full of little words like that aren't you! Yes, there is a fine line between managing my life and being happy with it. I have gotten tangled in it too many times to want to walk it again. Look, you've obviously gotten lucky— bad choice of words—had good fortune, with relationships. I have failed miserably. *(Pauses.)* I don't want to talk about this anymore—balanced by five—just let me work. *(Silence. Only the sounds of the office are heard. LOU halfheartedly attempts to work. RITA stares at the cubicle wall. Finally, RITA.)* People think they want me. They say they want me. They stay with me just long enough to convince me that they want me and convince me that I want..., need them too. And they leave.

LOU. Why do we have to think that far ahead? Why can't...

RITA. I have to! If I don't think ahead, I'll do it again. I'll think that I've found the right one again and then... nothing. I'll end up in bed again—crying until I'm too exhausted to cry. There have been weekends that I've fallen asleep in tears only to wake up with the energy to feel those agonies again. No other person goes through this kind of recycled torture. I don't get over things. Hell, I have more in common with Prometheus than I do any man I've dated in my lifetime! A mattress instead of a rock; apathies instead of vultures.

LOU. Time heals all wounds.

RITA. Stop that! It's those goofy little romantic sayings that destroy people like me. Time does not heal all wounds—it's not a absolute truth. You have to keep an eye on time. Its value decreases as your mishaps increase. Simple balance.

LOU. You were not screaming all this "simple balance" stuff last night and we had a great time.

RITA. No, I was screaming for the bartender last night and we did not have a great time, we had sex! Please get that through your mind.

(RITA checks her watch, and returns to scribbling. LOU stares at the wall in front of him, searching for the right words.)

LOU. Rita...

RITA. Balanced by five, Lou, balanced by five.

LOU. Put your hand up to mine.

(LOU leans over his desk and places his hand on the wall of the cubicle, noisily moving papers and such in the process.)

RITA. What?

LOU. Put your hand on the wall.

RITA. What are you doing over there? This is an office.

LOU. Place your hand on mine.

RITA. Sit down! People are going to see you, hear you!

LOU. I'm only going to get louder, Rita. Unless you put your hand on the wall.

RITA. Have you lost your mind?

LOU. *(Louder.)* Rita, put your hand...

RITA. All right. All right. All right.

(RITA quickly leans over and places one hand on the cubicle wall. THEY are still for a few seconds.)

LOU. Can you feel it? My hand?

RITA. I'm not sure. *(She thinks.)* I think I do.

LOU. Follow it to the top.

RITA. Lou, cut it out.

LOU. You got your say. Now I get mine.

RITA. People are going to see us!

LOU. No one is going to see. They are all in their separate boxes—Balanced by five, remember. Ready?

RITA. I don't know...

LOU. Go.

(THEY slowly run their hands up the cubicle in sync. BOTH grit their teeth and close their eyes in anticipation. Their hands meet above the wall. It is as if they had never touched before and the previous night pales in comparison. Their bodies are strewn across their desk and they can see nothing of each other save their fingertips.)

RITA. Wow. I can't believe I'm doing this.

LOU. Let's go for more.

RITA. This is too much for me to handle. Too fast.

LOU. Place your face beside mine.

RITA. I can't do that! I can't even reach.

LOU. Get up on your desk. Do it.

RITA. I can't...

LOU. Don't stop now. Don't talk, just do.

RITA. Okay. Okay. Okay. I'm doing it. I'm doing it. *(Still holding each other's hand above the cubicle, they make room for their bodies on top of their desks with their free hands. After clearing a space, they crawl on top of their desks.)* What am I doing?

LOU. *(Muffled by the cubicle wall.)* Remember where you felt my hand? Put your lips there. That's where mine are.

RITA. I'm willing to bet we could lose our jobs for this.

LOU. Do it!

RITA. *(Now muffled as well.)* I am. *(THEY freeze in the awkwardness. Silence.)* Now what?

LOU. Follow me up.

RITA. Wait, everyone will see.

LOU. When is the last time you checked for people crawling above your cubicle? Trust me. Follow me up.

(Slowly THEY drag their faces up the cubicle wall, lips puckered, eyes closed in hope. As they move upwards, they emit a slight sound, rising in pitch together. When they reach the top of the cubicle wall... nothing. They've missed each other, by inches. RITA opens her eyes.)

RITA. Oh God. Missed. What was I thinking?! *(She starts to crawl down. Dejected.)* Balanced by five.

LOU. Wait.

(LOU lifts her chin up and stops her from crawling down. As he pulls her face up, a gaze of wonderment comes over her. A new perspective. A feeling beyond the missed kiss, beyond disappointment.)

RITA. Look at everybody.

LOU. You can't even see their faces.

RITA. They're bored. Lonely, too. I thought they were always happy at their desks. They always look happy at the copier. They won't shut up about their dogs and cats and daughters in college. But from here they look still... lifeless... complacent.

LOU. Manageable.

(LOU kisses her. RITA kisses him.)

RITA. Look, ugh, *(She looks at her watch.)* it's two minutes to

five and I just don't think I'm going to get this account balanced, so
if you're still up for dinner...
    LOU. Wonderful. *(Looking at his disheveled desk below him.)*
Umm, I have some things on my desk I need to clear up and then I'll
be ready...

*(LOU crawls down from the desk, still holding her hand above the
    wall. He straightens papers, puts things away, etc. She remains
    seated on her desk, still holding on tight to LOU.)*

    RITA. No, no. I want to go now. I need to...

(RITA sneezes.)

    LOU. *(Quickly.)* God bless you.
    RITA. Thank you.

*(LOU sits down on his desk. THEY are still. Papers everywhere. Each
    holding the other's hand over the cubicle. Sounds of the office
    resume. Lights fade.)*

THE END

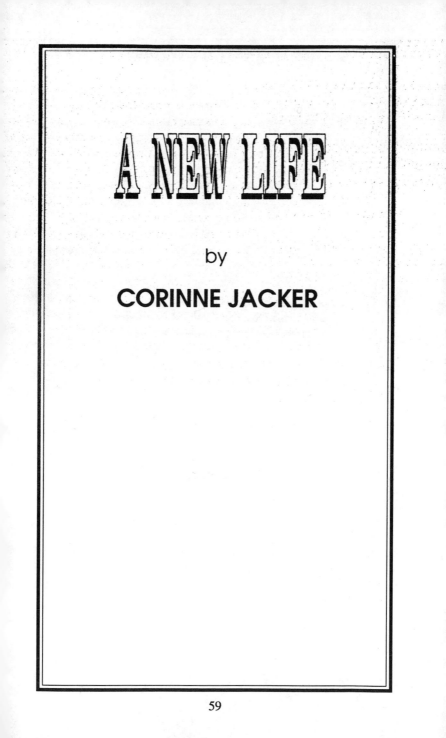

A NEW LIFE

by

CORINNE JACKER

A NEW LIFE
by **Corinne Jacker**
Directed by **John Cambell Finnegan**
Dramaturg: **Jeffrey Ullom**

Sol ....Rick Silverman
Tom ....Justin Hagan

Scenic Designer **Stephanie R. Gerckens**
Costume Designer **Kevin R. McLeod**
Lighting Designer **Kathleen Kronauer**
Sound Designer **Martin R. Desjardins**
Properties Designer **Mark Walston**
Stage Manager **Sarah Nicole Spearing**

A NEW LIFE

(The year is 1920. TOM, 20, dressed up in a suit, tie, etc., his hair pomaded and combed down, is ready for a date. SOL, 25, his brother, who has been sitting and reading the paper looks up when TOM speaks to him.)

TOM. Here. I got you this. *(He slams a heavy book down in front of SOL.)* Is it the one you wanted?

SOL. *(Examining the book.)* Oh, no Tom.

TOM. The other day, you were standing there, your nose pressed up against the book store window, like it was full of chocolate candy. I thought—if I got the wrong one, they said I could take it back.

SOL. No. That's the one I was looking at. But, Tommy, it cost so much. I won't be able to pay you back for a couple of weeks—

TOM. Forget it, Sol. It made me happy to do. Just say thank you. That's all I want to hear.

SOL. Of course, "thank you." Of course. It's wonderful.

(HE opens the book and starts reading.)

TOM. *The Opinions of Justice Holmes.* What do you need it for, Sol?

SOL. I don't *need* it. But you don't know Tommy—the things I can learn from it.

TOM. You don't need to learn. You're a lawyer already.

(SOL is absorbed by where he has begun to read.)

61

TOM. So how do I look?

SOL. You stink.

TOM. I don't. It's new stuff they got in at the barbershop. You put it on your hair and see, the curl is practically gone.

SOL. Who cares?

TOM. I do. She does.

SOL. Then she's nuts. You still stink. Wash it off so you smell like a human being. You don't have to get so dressed up for *shul.*

TOM. I'm not going to *shul.* I got invited to Tessie's for dinner.

SOL. It's *simchas torah.*

TOM. So? It'll be *simchas torah* without me.

SOL. You know the story about wine and Chelm. *(TOM shakes his head.)* The rabbi decided he was going to make sure the poor of Chelm would have wine for *kaddish* on the high holidays. So he had a barrel put in the entrance of the *shul.* And every *shabbos* the men were supposed to put a few drops of their wine in the barrel and when it was opened just before the high holidays, there would be enough for the poor. So everything went according to plan, and the barrel was full when the *shamus* took it down and opened it. Except instead of wine, it was full of water. Every man thought his few drops of water wouldn't hurt anything. *(Pause.)* Tommy. Your absence hurts something.

TOM. You don't need me. A *minyan* isn't personal. Yank some guy in off the street.

SOL. And dad? What's he supposed to think?

TOM. Oh, yeah. He cares. He comes here with the first boatload, and he leaves ma and me and the kids to run the farm. All we hear from you guys is when you have the ticket money to send us over steerage.

SOL. We worked plenty hard for that money.

TOM. Doing what?

SOL. None of your business... So maybe we cut a few corners to get it.

TOM. I don't care. You could have robbed a bank for all it matters to me. Now I work hard.

SOL. You don't know what hard work is. I've always held it against you—getting the soft job in the match factory, when we worked there as kids. You were the sweet little boy, so all you had to do was paste the labels on the match boxes. Me! The big boy! The *macher*, I get to really work, cutting the matches for hours. Now you call it work— they take care of you like you were a girl!

TOM. Yeah? I carried a bathtub up two flights today. By myself. You sit and read these thick books— *(He hefts the book he bought SOL.)* Oh sure, that's heavy work. You might get a hernia, Sol. Now. I sweat enough. I got one day off. I want to enjoy it. Pop can think what he wants.

(Pause.)

SOL. Tessie lives all the way across the park. You taking a bus?

TOM. I'm not walking. Don't look at me like that. I know it's after sunset. I know what laws I'm breaking. And I'll tell you something. That dinner won't be kosher. So add another sin. In a couple of weeks I get a new page in the book of life.

SOL. What do you care? Sometimes I think you aren't even a Jew anymore.

TOM. I'm an American Jew. Not like you and your brothers and dad. I talk American, I dress American, I want to live like an American. I can even fox trot now. I'm a citizen. I voted Republican for the whole ticket last time.

SOL. You forget who you are? Where we came from? If Benny hadn't got sent to Siberia with Trotsky, we'd still be on the farm milking cows.

TOM. Benny may be an orthodox Jew, but he voted Republican, too. I got told who I am by customs when we got off the boat. The guy asked my name, and I told him. Yankl. He couldn't understand me. I couldn't spell my name his way. So he wrote down Thomas. So that's my name now. Even you don't call me Yankl, do you?

SOL. All the pogroms over there. We lived. We lived to be Jews. To be free in America, to be Jews.

TOM. Sol, in America, I'm going to be free to be rich, to eat steak and drink all the beer I want, not have radishes night after night because that's all there is. I see how Tessie's father lives. He knows what's what.

SOL. Tommy, he makes his money taking kickbacks in the court.

TOM. So. It's money. It buys things.

SOL. Like Tessie, is that living? Like a *shiksa* is how she lives. She puts polish on her nails. Her dresses are short. The way she looks at men. Women don't look at men like that.

TOM. Where we were, they didn't, not in the *shtetl.* Here the rules are different. No *shtetl* no ghetto.

SOL. Maybe it's too much. You grew up a good Jew. You can be a good Jew here.

TOM. A good Jew has *pais.* Why don't you have *pais.*

SOL. *(Mumbling.)* You know why.

TOM. No I don't. Tell me. Come on. I want to know.

SOL. Shut up!

TOM. The lawyers at Klein, Sacher, and Moritz never would have hired you if you had *pais*, would they? American courts, American lawyers can't go into courts in *pais.*

SOL. So. To me it's a costume. Inside I'm still who I was. What's the harm if I want to look like the other lawyers?

TOM. No harm. And there's no harm if I let some of the other things go.

SOL. You're letting everything go... You make me sick. You don't act like us. You don't think like us. Why don't you do like Abe Rosen did? On the next job application, where it says "Religion" just put Christian Scientist.

TOM. ... If I tell you something, you won't tell pop?

SOL. Why would I run to pop? It's your life. You want to walk away from us, walk. Run. Just don't look back because the door's gonna be closed.

TOM. Come on. A few harmless things—

SOL. The black candles will be lit. You'll be read out of the *shul.* No one will talk to you. Then pop'll know. Then he'll cry until he's dead.

TOM. For God's sake—

SOL. Aha! You even take the Lord's name in vain.

TOM. All I was going to tell you—I went out with the boss, Mr. Gunner, and some of the supervisors. We were celebrating my getting my journeyman card.

SOL. I know. He's *goyim.* So you didn't eat kosher. You don't anymore.

TOM. I had a lobster. *(SOL is shocked.)* Shrimp cocktail to start and then a lobster. No bolt of lightning to strike me dead. I didn't get sick. It tasted funny, but I liked the taste; it tasted like a new life. You don't understand. I'm sick of being a greenhorn, of the other guys making fun of me. You remember how it was? When I went to my first dance and didn't know how to fox trot. How they clapped when I got through it and one of them offered me a kosher chocolate bar. It had a funny chalky taste, but I figured this was American food, and to be one of the crowd, I ate the whole thing. The whole bar of Ex-Lax. I got such cramps. They laughed. Dumb kike, didn't even know candy from a laxative. Nobody laughs at me any more. I learned. I can drink beer like anyone else, and I know the names of the Chicago Cubs and how to play baseball. The other night, I won $2.00 at poker—I won! Do you know how to play poker?

SOL. Who cares?

TOM. They do. They care if we can do what they do.

SOL. It won't get you into their clubs, their fancy restaurants, even their houses. I'm smart enough to know that. You can imitate them like a monkey, but that doesn't make you a real *shagitz*.

TOM. Oh, you may be the genius. You got through college and law school and you're a big lawyer. I only got through eighth grade and I'm just a plumber. But who makes more money? Who sees dinner gets on the table every night? Who's making sure ma has a dress and the kids have shoes that fit 'em?

SOL. Better we should all go barefoot.

TOM. Oh, yeah, you haven't turned down anything I brought into the house yet. You eat my food, and then you walk your Socialist picket lines.

SOL. And you don't put all your money into things for the family. You buy flowers and candy for your girlfriend.

TOM. Don't start telling me how to spend my money. Sally got a toy last week, and Freddy. Dad made wine last week. This family is going to survive. I'm going to be rich. I'm gonna marry Tessie and have a house and belong to a club and live like I belong here.

SOL. Don't let him hear you.

TOM. Dad? He doesn't even speak English.

SOL. What's wrong with that?

TOM. It's fine as long as I support him. Talking Yiddish, praying as what we did in the old country. When they didn't kill us and rape the women. Sol, we're in America now. You brought us here. Americans don't pray, not all the time; they work and make money.

SOL. Capitalist!

TOM. Socialist!

SOL. Shhhh!

TOM. Praying isn't going to get Tessie what she wants.

SOL. Tessie. Her father was born in Vienna. He always thought he was more German than Jew. She comes from another world.

TOM. *(Very appreciatively.)* Yeah. She's classy.

SOL. *(Sarcastically.)* Classy.

TOM. Get some brains, will you.

SOL. Classy! Fancy! Rich! Money! Every other word that comes out of your mouth is about that.

TOM. Why'd you come over here, anyway? Why don't you go back where you came from? It's people like you who give us a bad name.

SOL. Listen to you! If they had secret police, you'd turn us in.

TOM. Shit!

SOL. You can even swear like an American.

TOM. They all do, on the job.

SOL. You think you can have it all. But you'll have to pick, Tommy, us or them. You'll have kids, and you'll die, and they won't even know to say kaddish or light a *yartzeit* candle. And they'll have kids who don't know any Hebrew and soon, what we came here to save will be all gone, thrown away like dish water.

TOM. It's not going to come to that. I just want to keep my head above water.

SOL. *(SOL closes the book and gives it back to TOM.)* I'm not going to help you lose your soul. Here. Take it back. Buy Tessie a fan or something!

TOM. Hey! No! It was a present. For you. Keep it.

SOL. I'll buy it when I can afford it.

TOM. Which'll be never.

SOL. I said I don't want the book. I don't want your damn charity!

TOM. You didn't have any trouble taking it before. Take my advice. Save your big morals till you can afford them.

(He tries to hand the book back to SOL.)

SOL. I don't want it!
TOM. Neither do I. what would I do with it?

(The two tussle over the book at first gently, then a little more violently. Finally, it falls to the floor with a bang.)

TOM. Okay. Eat the damn book for supper. That's all it's good for.

(TOM walks slowly out of the room, whistling, slams the door behind him. SOL sits, looking after him, then picks up the books, smooths out a few pages and begins to read. TOM's whistle, of a popular tune, can still be faintly heard.)

THE END

OFF THE RACK

by
ROBERT D. KEMNITZ
and
JENNIFER McMASTER

OFF THE RACK
by **Robert D. Kemnitz** and **Jennifer McMaster**

Directed by **Victoria Norman Brown**
Dramaturg **Corby Tushla**

Pauline	Suzan Mikiel
Adrienne	Michelle Tomko

Scenic Designer **Stephanie R. Gerckens**
Costume Designer **Kevin R. McLeod**
Lighting Designer **Kathleen Kronauer**
Sound Designer **Martin R. Desjardins**
Properties Designer **Mark Walston**
Stage Manager **Sarah Nicole Spearing**

OFF THE RACK

(Lights Up: A large walk-in closet. The only set piece is a large pole running the length of the stage, crammed with every item of clothing known to woman, hung from one side to the other.)

(AT RISE: PAULINE is sorting her outfits. In reality she is moving them back and forth with limited results.)

PAULINE. Let's see, let's see, long sleeve, long sleeve, long sleeve, short sleeve. Oh, no no no, that will never do. Let's put you over here, no, that's blazers. Blazers and suits. Blazers and suits and skirts. Oh, I remember this one. The look on their faces when I...

(She puts first item back, and pulls down a wrap-around skirt, which, as she finds, no longer wraps around.)

PAULINE. Another two weeks at the gym should fix that. Let's see, where was I? Oh, how much time do I have? Damn. Where did that blouse go? Let's see, evening wear—no, that's somewhat-formal wear. Ooh, that's the jacket that goes with the slacks that go with that silk blouse that I wore to my first...

(She pulls down a jacket and tries to close it in front of her.)

PAULINE. Going to have to step up on the Slim Fast. That's fine, that's fine. Let's see, let's see. We have purple, purple, that's almost purple, that's not. Oh, that's the dress—I love that dress.

(She pulls down a dress and tries to pull it over her head. She gets stuck.)

PAULINE. Not even an act of God.

(The doorbell rings.)

PAULINE She's here! *(Calling from beneath the dress.)* Door's open!

(PAULINE struggles to get the dress off her head. After a moment, ADRIENNE enters. Her movements, dress and speech are sharp. There is nothing extraneous about her.)

ADRIENNE. Good afternoon. I'm Adrienne Proctor. Proctor Personal Services.
PAULINE. I'm so glad you're here.

(ADRIENNE reaches to shake hands with PAULINE, who reaches out her hand, still holding the dress. ADRIENNE rips the dress from her hands, whips a plastic garbage bag from her purse and immediately deposits the dress in the bag.)

PAULINE. My dress—?
ADRIENNE. Let's be clear about one thing. I'm very good, I'm very expensive and you are paying by the hour. I was told this was an emergency, and I can see now that I was well informed. We're going to have to get to work right away.
PAULINE. Would you like a cup of tea?
ADRIENNE. Never bring beverages near your clothing. *(ADRIENNE walks past PAULINE, directly to the clothing rack.)* I see we've been trying to sort things through ourselves.
PAULINE. I just tidied up a few things.
ADRIENNE. Last ditch efforts are never a substitute for professional organization.
PAULINE. Well, I just thought I'd—
ADRIENNE. Don't—
PAULINE. —get started so you wouldn't—
ADRIENNE. Organization is not about thought. It's about remov-

ing thought. For the next four hours, try to keep from thinking anything. It will make my job much easier.

PAULINE. I'll try to keep that in mind.

ADRIENNE. Marvelous. Okay, Pauline, is it? Right. What is it that you want me to do?

PAULINE. I thought I explained over the phone...

ADRIENNE. Please, say it again. In front of the wardrobe.

PAULINE. I—I don't know what you—

ADRIENNE. Please state exactly the service you wish me to provide.

PAULINE. I... I want you to organize my closet.

ADRIENNE. Louder please.

PAULINE. I want you to organize my closet.

ADRIENNE. Good. It is very important to admit you have a problem. Now don't worry. That was the hardest thing you'll have to do. The rest is up to me. All the hard decisions. So when clothes start crying out to you, just remember—they won't hate you. They'll hate me.

PAULINE. Okay.

ADRIENNE. My motto: Chuck it all and let Goodwill sort it out. Say it.

PAULINE. *(Meekly.)* Chuck it all and let Goodwill sort it out.

ADRIENNE. Good. Now we can get started. You certainly have accumulated a high volume of worthless outfits.

PAULINE. It's a passion?

ADRIENNE. It's a disease. Judging from your stock, you've had the illness a long time. I bet you even keep all your toys and dolls from your childhood.

PAULINE. Of course I do. All of my old Barbie dolls, I must have forty of them—I remember, I had to have every single one of them, as soon as they came out—Malibu Barbie, Tahiti Barbie, Retro Barbie. I had to have them all.

ADRIENNE. Ah, yes. The Barbie Fantasy School of Clotheshopping. One party, one outfit. Another party, another outfit.

PAULINE. Yes, that's it exactly.

ADRIENNE. Well, some of us were able to select three or four neutral Barbie outfits to mix and match, giving her an endless array of stylish yet versatile ensembles. You see, Pauline, it's not so much what you wear, but how, and in your case, if you wear it.

PAULINE. Yes, yes. I see.

ADRIENNE. Let's get one thing straight. I may be brutal, I may appear unfeeling. And I am. And that's what you need.

PAULINE. All right.

ADRIENNE. I have three rules. If you haven't worn it in two months, it gets put aside. If you haven't worn it in six months, it gets considered. If you haven't worn it in nine months, it gets tossed.

PAULINE. You are tough.

ADRIENNE. Yes. I am. Let's have a look at the culprits. *(ADRIENNE stands at one end of the rack, and begins thumbing through the items. As she thumbs through.)* No, no, no, no, definitely not, no, no, no, fuschia? I don't think so, no, no, no, no, no, maybe— maybe not, and no.

(ADRIENNE grabs a stack of clothes off the rack and immediately stuffs them into her trash bag.)

PAULINE. Wait a minute! What are you doing?

ADRIENNE. I'm doing you a favor. *(Looking at the tag of one item.)* Size 6? Please.

PAULINE. I'm on a diet.

ADRIENNE. You and the rest of my clients. May I proceed?

PAULINE. Yes.

ADRIENNE. *(Finding another item.)* Size 8? Still optimistic, are we?

PAULINE. I've been working out.

ADRIENNE. One, Two, And Lift That Twinkie. Let's see, what else do we have? *(Finds another.)* Size 10? Reality begins slowly to set in.

PAULINE. I wore that last year to the Christmas party.

ADRIENNE. And I'm Elle McPherson. Let me guess, you're big-boned?

PAULINE. Well, my mother was...

ADRIENNE. It goes. It all goes.

(ADRIENNE takes another large bundle of clothes and tosses them in the garbage bag.)

ADRIENNE. You've eaten yourself right out of Chanel and into Lane Bryant.

(ADRIENNE pulls another dress and starts to throw it out.)

PAULINE. Oh, no. Not that one! Please, anything but that.

ADRIENNE. What is it—your prom dress?

PAULINE. I know I can wear that one again. It's my favorite.

ADRIENNE. And it hasn't fit you since 1985. It goes.

PAULINE. It doesn't!

ADRIENNE. It goes or I go.

PAULINE. *(Pause.)* Okay.

ADRIENNE. Very good. Here, have a cookie. *(ADRIENNE offers PAULINE a cookie from her shoulder bag. PAULINE accepts it, grudgingly.)* Every time you part with an item of sentimental or other value, you get a cookie.

PAULINE. But why do—

ADRIENNE. If you question me, you do not get a cookie.

PAULINE. Cookies aren't exactly on my diet.

ADRIENNE. Apparently you aren't exactly on your diet, either. Fair?

PAULINE. Fair. *(During the following, ADRIENNE pulls items off the shelf, looks to PAULINE for a verdict and hands her a cookie at the same time. Then ADRIENNE tosses the articles of clothing.)* Oh, Get rid of that one. *(Toss.)* What was I thinking? *(Toss.)* The blue one or the green one?

ADRIENNE. Neither.

(Toss. Toss.)

PAULINE. I was thinking of this one for my promotion interview next Wednesday.

ADRIENNE. What did I tell you about thinking?

PAULINE. Maybe you could make a suggestion?

ADRIENNE. Law firm, right?

PAULINE. Yes.

ADRIENNE. Straight dark skirt, high-neck blouse, cravat, navy blue blazer. You do have shoes?

PAULINE. Other closet.

ADRIENNE. That will be next week.

PAULINE. I don't know where I got all these clothes.

ADRIENNE. Saks, Lord and Taylors, Nordstrom...

PAULINE. I always loved dress-up.

ADRIENNE. Pauline, your dress-up days are over.

PAULINE. I just want to be my own life-size Barbie.

ADRIENNE. If you were a life-sized Barbie, you wouldn't be able to stand up straight. You'd have hired a chiropractor, not a Proctor Organizer.

PAULINE. Barbie was the prettiest woman I knew as a little girl. And Ken the handsomest man.

ADRIENNE. *(Holding something up.)* This?

PAULINE. Chuck it. *(She tosses the item herself.)* I had the perfect Barbie wedding planned—it was to be outdoors, in the Spring, all my friends were invited, the soundtrack to "Grease" playing in the background, and a honeymoon in the Dream House.

ADRIENNE. My Barbie never got married—she couldn't even get a date.

PAULINE. Everything was going to be just beautiful. I'd collected rose petals to spread on the patio, there was a gentle breeze, everyone looked perfect. And Ken stood her up. We waited for hours. No Ken. Barbie was crushed—she had her wedding gown on, complete with gold tiara. And Ken just never showed.

ADRIENNE. How awful.

PAULINE. Turns out, Ken had been abducted by my dog Spitfire the night before and buried alive. Buried alive!

ADRIENNE. It's those moments that shape us. Those early traumas. My best girlfriend growing up never had the Crayola 64—she just had the 8 fat boring dull colors. To this day, she can't coordinate colors to save her soul.

PAULINE. *(Returning to the rack.)* I wish I had that excuse. I mean, look at this outfit? Seventy-six dollars and just look at it.

ADRIENNE. No. It has a certain rustic charm to it.

PAULINE. Laura Ashley is the demon incarnate.

ADRIENNE. No, really, some of her prints are acceptable.

PAULINE. If you say so.

ADRIENNE. I do. I do. In fact... *(She searches in the garbage bag and pulls out a skirt.)* ... I think I was too quick to judge this one. It has a... je ne sais quoi... an appeal. I thought I'd never see this color again, but I've heard rumors that fuschia is going to make a comeback.

PAULINE. I always though that was the perfect thing for Valentine's Day.

ADRIENNE. *(Searching through the bag.)* With just a few accessories. Studded belt, oh definitely. Lavender turtleneck. And anklets. Hot pink anklets—that will really turn heads.

PAULINE. Yes! Yes!

ADRIENNE. *(Suddenly dropping clothes.)* What am I saying?

PAULINE. I have some lime green anklets, would that work better?

ADRIENNE. I feel dizzy.

PAULINE. And—dare I say—one of those hippie rope bracelets?

ADRIENNE. Stop! Stop right now! I can't breathe!

PAULINE. Miss Proctor, is everything all right?

ADRIENNE. No, everything is not all right. I've lost my faculties. My fashion senses have left me. I'm too close.

PAULINE. Well, stand over here. It all looks great to me.

ADRIENNE. You don't understand. In my profession, objectivity is everything. I'm losing my discerning eye.

PAULINE. I think you're doing a great job. Let's keep going!

ADRIENNE. I can't see the forest greens for the aquas. I have to get out of here!

PAULINE. Don't go! We're having so much fun!

ADRIENNE. Fashion should never be fun! I have to leave, I must get out of this—this vacuum! I'll recommend one of my associates. I have to leave this place now.

PAULINE. But—?

ADRIENNE. I'm so ashamed.

(ADRIENNE exits quickly. PAULINE is left to her own devices. She looks around the room, heart-broken.)

PAULINE. Well, fine—who needs you.

(PAULINE grabs an item off the rack with every intention of throwing it in the bag. But she pauses, looks at it, then places it back on the rack.)

PAULINE. Fuschia? Well, yes. I think it is about time.

(She reaches for the bag. Blackout.)

THE END

REVERSE TRANSCRIPTION

Six Playwrights Bury a Seventh
A Ten-Minute Play That's Nearly
Twenty Minutes Long

by

TONY KUSHNER

REVERSE TRANSCRIPTION was first performed at the 1996 Humana Festival of New American Plays, March, 1996. It was directed by **Tony Kushner** with the following cast::

Hautflote.. John Leonard Thompson
Aspera ....Jennifer Hubbard
Biff ....Daniel Oreskes
Happy ....Christopher Evan Welch
Ottoline ....Fanni Green
Flatty ....Fred Major
Ding

Production Staff

Scenic Designer **Paul Owen**
Costume Designer **Kevin R. McLeod**
Lighting Designer **T.J. Gerckens**
Sound Designer **Martin R. Desjardins**
Properties Manager **Ron Riall**
Stage Manager **Cind Senensieb**
Dramaturg **Liz Engelman**
New York Casting Arrangements **Laura Richin Casting**

CHARACTERS

HAUTFLOTE: A playwright in his late thirties. He writes beautiful plays everyone admires; he has a following and little financial success. He was Ding's best friend, the executor of his will and his wishes.

ASPERA: A playwright in her early thirties. She writes fierce splendidly intelligent challenging plays, frequently with lesbian characters, and cannot get an American theater to produce her for love or money. So she lives in London where she is acclaimed. She is cool and is beginning to sound British.

BIFF: A playwright in his late thirties. Scruffy, bisexual, one success, several subsequent failures, cannot stay away from political themes though his analysis is not rigorous. He is overdue; he should be home, writing; he should not be here.

HAPPY: A playwright in his late thirties. His early plays were widely admired, then one big success and he's become a Hollywood writer, TV mostly, rich now, a little bored, but very happy. He plans to go back to writing for the theater someday.

OTTOLINE: A playwright in her fifties. African-American, genuinely great hugely influential experimentalist whom everyone adores but who is now languishing in relative obscurity and neglect, though she continues to write prolifically. She is the best writer of the bunch and the least well remunerated. Hers is a deep bitterness; the surface is immensely gracious. She teaches playwrights and has a zoological fascination, watching them. Ding was her protégé, sort of. She is an old friend of Flatty's.

FLATTY: A playwright in his late forties. Colossally rich. An easy target for negativity of all kinds though he is in fact a good writer, hugely prolific, very hard-working and generous to his fellow 'wrights.

DING. A dead playwright wrapped in a winding sheet. A very talented writer, whom everyone admired for wildly different reasons.

PLACE

A cemetery on Abel's Hill, Martha's Vineyard, in December near midnight.

NOTE:

Abel's Hill is a real place, a spectacularly beautiful mostly 19th Century Yankee graveyard; it's way to expensive for any mortal to get a plot in it now. Lillian Hellman and Dashiell Hammett are buried there. So is John Belushi, whose tombstone kept getting stolen by fans til Dan Ackroyd put a gigantic boulder on Belushi's grave, too huge for anyone to lift. From the crest of the hill you can see the ocean.

Everyone has shovels, and several have bottles of various liquors. The night is beautiful and very cold.

They are writers so they love words. Their speech is precise, easy, articulate; they are showing off a little. They are at that stage of drunk, right before sloppy, where you are eloquent, impressing yourself. They are making pronouncements, aware of their wit; this mustn't be pinched, crabbed, dour, effortful. They are having fun on this mad adventure; they relish its drama. Underneath is a very deep grief.

They all really loved Ding.

REVERSE TRANSCRIPTION

(High atop Abel's Hill, a cemetery on Martha's Vineyard. Just athwart the crest. Tombstones all around. As the voice of the playwright is heard on tape, with an accompanying obbligato of a typewriter's clattering, BIFF, HAPPY, ASPERA, OTTOLINE and FLATTY gather, facing downhill. HAUTFLOTE appears, carrying the body of DING, wrapped in a winding sheet. HAUTFLOTE places the body before them, then runs off, then returns with six shovels. The other playwrights look about uneasily, and then sit. They have come to bury him illegally. It's nearly midnight.)

THE VOICE OF THE PLAYWRIGHT. DRAMATIS PERSO-NAE. Seven characters, all playwrights. Biff, scruffy, bisexual, one success, several subsequent failures, cannot stay away from political themes though his analysis is not rigorous. He is overdue; he should be home, writing; he should not be here. Happy, his early plays were widely admired, then one big success and he's become a Hollywood writer, TV mostly, rich now, a little bored, but very... um, well, happy. He plans to go back to writing for the theater someday. Aspera writes fierce splendidly intelligent challenging plays, frequently with lesbian characters, and she cannot get an American theater to produce her for love or money. So she lives in London where she is acclaimed. Ottoline, African-American, genuinely great hugely influential experimentalist whom everyone adores but who is now languishing in relative obscurity and neglect, the best writer of the bunch and the least well remunerated. She is an old friend of Flatty, colossally successful. Colossally rich. An easy target for negativity of all kinds though he is in fact a good writer, hugely prolific. Hautflote writes beautiful experimental plays, has a small loyal following and little

83

financial success; the best friend and the executor of the estate of Ding, a dead playwright wrapped in a winding sheet, very talented, whom everyone admired for wildly different reasons. Seven characters are too many for a ten-minute play. It'll be twenty minutes long! Fuck it. One of them is dead and the others can all talk fast. The play takes place in Abel's Hill cemetery, a spectacularly beautiful, mostly 19th Century Yankee graveyard, way too expensive for any mortal to get a plot in it now. On Abel's Hill, Martha's Vineyard, in December near midnight.

(When the voice is finished, HAUTFLOTE goes to a nearby headstone, on the side of which is a light switch. He flicks it on; a full moon appears in the sky.

HAUTFLOTE. Ah!

(The play begins.)

HAUTEFLOTE. Here. We should start digging.

ASPERA. Athwart the crest. Facing the sea. As Ding demanded.

OTTOLINE. Isn't this massively illegal?

FLATTY. Trespass, destruction of private property, destruction of a historical landmark I shouldn't wonder, conveyance of tissue, i.e. poor Ding, in an advanced state of morbidity, on public transportation...

HAUTFLOTE. He's been *preserved.* He's hazardous to no one's health. *(Small pause.)* He traveled here in a steamer trunk. The porters helped.

BIFF. *(Apostrophizing.)* O please come to me short sweet simple perfect *idea.* A seed, a plot.

HAUTFLOTE. He's under a deadline.

BIFF. I'm doomed.

HAUTFLOTE. Now shoulder your shovels...

BIFF. There's no dignity, have you noticed? In being *this.* An American playwright. What is that?

OTTOLINE. Well, we drink.

HAPPY. No one really drinks now. None of us, at least not publicly.

FLATTY. I can't remember something.
HAPPY. We're...

(HAPPY is looking for the word.)

FLATTY. A name.
HAPPY. Healthier!
HAUTFLOTE. What name?
FLATTY. The name of the country that makes me despair.
HAPPY. But tonight we are drunk.
BIFF. In honor of Ding.
HAUTFLOTE. What letter does it begin with?
BIFF. Poor Ding.

(They ALL look at DING. Little pause.)

ASPERA. "And Poor Ding Who Is Dead."

(Little pause.)

FLATTY. R.
HAUTFLOTE. Rwanda.
FLATTY. *That's* it.
OTTOLINE. How could you *forget*, Flatty? Rwanda?
FLATTY. I've never had a head for names. Not in the news much, anymore, Rwanda.
OTTOLINE. We are afraid to stick the shovel in.
HAUTFLOTE. Yes.
OTTOLINE. Believing it to be a desecration.
HAUTFLOTE. Of this holy earth.
OTTOLINE. Not *holy*: Pure. Authentic.
HAPPY. Yankee.
OTTOLINE. Pilgrim.
HAPPY. Puritan.
OTTOLINE. Originary. Forefatherly.
ASPERA. Oh fuck me, "forefatherly"; John Belushi's buried here!
FLATTY. And he had enough drugs in him when he died to poison all the waters from here to Nantucket.

OTTOLINE. And the people steal his tombstone.

FLATTY. No!

OTTOLINE. Or the hill keeps swallowing it up. It doesn't rest in peace. A pretender, you see.

ASPERA. Lillian Hellman's buried here. She's a playwright.

HAUTFLOTE. Appropriate or no it's what Ding wanted.

OTTOLINE. And that's another thing. It cost two hundred thirty seven dollars and fifty cents for a round trip ticket. From New York. This is an *island*. Martha's Vineyard is an *island*! Did Ding *realize* that? One has to *ferry* across. Fucking Ding. Maybe *you all* have money. For ferry passage. I don't have money. I've got no money.

FLATTY. I told you I'd pay for you.

OTTOLINE. Well we all know *you've* got money.

BIFF. O come to me short sweet simple idea!

FLATTY. I want something magical to happen.

BIFF. A plot. The Horseleech hath two daughters. It's a start. And these daughters... Do... What?

HAPPY. They cry!

OTTOLINE. Give, give!

BIFF. Brecht in exile circumnavigated the globe. Berlin. Skovbostrand. Stockholm. Helsinki. Leningrad. Moscow. Vladivostock. Manila. L.A.. Quick stop in D.C. to visit the HUAC. New York. Paris. Zurich. Salzburg. Prague. Berlin. An American playwright, what is that? Never in exile, always in extremis. The list of cities: AIDS, loss, fear of infection, unsafe sex he says gazing upon the corpse of a fallen comrade, I fuck men and women. I dream my favorite actor has been shot by the police, I dream I shoot Jesse Helms in the head and it doesn't kill him...

FLATTY. Eeewww, *politics.*

BIFF. I dream we are intervening in Bosnia merely to give Germany hegemony over Eastern Europe. Why, I dream myself in my dream asking myself, do you dream that? You do not dream a play, you *write* a play. And this play is due, and there's *(Pointing to DING's corpse.)* the deadline. I write in my notebook that I am glad we are sending troops to former Yugoslavia but I *(He makes the "in quotes" gesture with his fingers.)* "inadvertently" spell troops "T-R-O-U-P-E-S" as in troupes as in theatrical troupes, traveling players, we are sending *troupes* to former Yugoslavia.

HAUTFLOTE. I don't think we can avoid it any longer. The digging.

FLATTY. I imagine it's worth serious jail time for us all.

HAPPY. Incarcerated playwrights. Now *that* has dignity. Until it's learned what for.

BIFF. I repulse myself, I am not of this earth, if I were more serious I would be an essayist if I were more observant a novelist more articulate more intelligent a poet more... succinct more *ballsy* a screenwriter and then I could buy an apartment.

HAUTFLOTE. Fuck the public. It's all Ding asked for. He never got his own, alive.

ASPERA. Poor poor Ding.

HAUTFLOTE. He grew obsessed with his cemetery, in his final months. We visited it years ago. On a day trip, we could never afford... to *stay* here. Or anywhere. Or anything. Health Insurance. "Bury me on Abel's Hill." His final words. I think he thought this place would give him a retroactive pedigree.

OTTOLINE. That's it, *pedigree*, not *holiness*. Blood, genes. Of which we playwrights are envious. We're mutts. Amphibians.

ASPERA. Not of the land not of the sea. Not of the page nor of the moment.

HAPPY. Perdurable page. Fleeting moment.

FLATTY. Something magical should happen now.

HAUTFLOTE. Ding wanted to belong. Or rather, he never wanted not to. Or rather he never didn't want to, he *wanted* to not want to, but did. In his final months he grew finical.

ASPERA. When I saw him he wasn't finical, he was horrible. He looked horrible and he screamed at everyone all day and all night and there was no way he could get warm, ever. It was quite a change. I hadn't seen him in months, I was visiting from London WHERE I LIVE, IN *EXILE*, PRODUCED, APPLAUDED, *LAUDED* EVEN and NO ONE IN AMERICA WILL *TOUCH* MY WORK, but anyway he was somehow very very angry but not bitter. One felt envied, but not blamed. At Ding's deathbed.

HAUTFLOTE. Ding Bat. Der Dingle. Ding-An-Sich

HAPPY. I remember being impressed when I learned that the HIV virus, which has robbed us of our Ding, reads and writes its genetic alphabets backwards, RNA transcribing DNA transcribing RNA, hence *retro*virus, reverse transcription. I'm not gay but I am a Jew and so of course I, too, "read backwards, write backwards"; I think of Hebrew.

FLATTY. You're not gay?

HAPPY. No.

FLATTY. You're *not*?

HAPPY. No.

FLATTY. Everyone things you are. Everyone wants to sleep with you. Everyone. *Everyone*. Oops. You were saying?

HAPPY. I was saying that in my grief I thought... Well here I attempt a metaphor doomed to fail... I mean here we are, playwrights in a graveyard, here to dig, right? So, digging, I think: HIV, reverse transcribing, dust to dust, writing backwards, Hebrew and the Great and Terrible magic of that backwards alphabet, which runs against the grain, counter to the current of European tradition, heritage, thought: a language of fiery, consuming revelation, of refusal, the proper way, so I was taught, to address oneself to God... *(He puts his hands on DING's body.)* Perhaps, maybe, this backwards-writing viral nightmare is keeping some secret, subterraneanly affianced to a principle of... Reversals: good reversals and also very bad, where good meets bad, perhaps, the place of mystery where back meets forth, where our sorrow's not the point, where the forward flow of life brutally throws itself into reverse, to reveal... *(He lies alongside the body, curls up to it, head on DING's shoulder, listening.)* What? Hebrew always looked to me like zipper teeth unzipped. What awesome thing is it we're zipping open? To what do we return when we write in reverse? What's relinquished, what's released? What does it sound like I'm doing here?

ASPERA. It sounds like you're equating Hebrew and AIDS.

HAPPY. I'm...

ASPERA. I'm not Jewish but I am a dyke and I think either way, AIDS equals Hebrew or the reverse, you're in BIG trouble. I'm going to beat you up.

HAPPY. Not *equals*, I... I'm lonely. I'm among playwrights. Back East for the first time in months. So I get to talk. And none of you listen anyway. In Culver City everyone listens, they listen listen listen. They take notes. They take you at your word. You are playwrights. So be inattentive. If you paid attention you'd be novelists.

FLATTY. Aspera has spent five years in London. She's acquired the listening disease.

OTTOLINE. Soon, unless she watches herself, she will be an American playwright no longer but British, her plays will be all nuance, inference.

FLATTY. Yes, nuance, unless she's careful, or a socialist feminist.

BIFF. Everyone hates you Flatty.

OTTOLINE. Oops.

FLATTY. *(Unfazed, not missing a beat.)* And then there will be no nuance at all.

ASPERA. *Does* everyone hate you?

FLATTY. No, they don't.

ASPERA. I live in London now, I'm out of the loop.

FLATTY. They don't hate me, they envy me my money.

ASPERA. *(To HAPPY.)* I wouldn't *really* beat you up.

FLATTY. I could buy and sell the lot of you. Even *you*, Happy and *you write sitcoms.* There I've said it. I am wealthy. My plays have made me wealthy. I am richer than essayists, novelists, at least the respectable ones, and all poets ever. Envy is rather *like* hatred but as it's more debilitating to its votaries and votaresses (because it's so inherently undignified) it's of less danger ultimately to its targets.

BIFF. I don't envy your money. I envy your reviews.

HAUTFLOTE. I think we should dig now and bury Ding. This ground is patrolled. The night doesn't last forever. Ding's waiting.

OTTOLINE. *(Softly, firmly.)* Ding's dead. I love this place. It was worth two hundred and thirty seven dollars and fifty cents to get here. Yes Flatty you can pay my way. Send me a check. Biff's got a point. It's the reviews, isn't it. I've worked tirelessly for decades. Three at least. What I have done no one has ever done and no one does it nearly so well. But what I do is break the vessels because they never fit me right and I despise their elegance and I like the sound the breaking makes, it's a new music. What I do is make mess apparent or make apparent messes, I cannot tell which myself I signal disenfranchisement, dysfunction, disinheritance well I *am* a black woman what do they expect it's hard stuff but it's life but I am *perverse* I do not want my stories straight up the narrative the narrative the miserable fucking narrative the universe is post-Cartesian post-Einsteinian it's not at any rate what it's post-to-be let's throw some curve balls already who cares if they never cross the plate it's hard too hard for folks to apprehend easy so I get no big money review and no box office and I'm broke, I'm fifty or sixty or maybe I've turned eighty, I collected the box at the Cafe Cinno yes I am THAT old, and poor but no matter, I have a great talent for poverty. Oblivion, on the other hand, scares me. Death. And this may shock you but *(To FLATTY.)* I ENVY you... your RENOWN. *(Roaring.) I DON'T WANT ANOTHER OBIE! I want a hit! I want to hit a home run! I WANT A MARQUEE!* I'm too old to be ashamed of my hunger.

BIFF. O come to me short sweet. *(He blows a raspberry.)* There's just no dignity. I am oppressed by theatre critics.

FLATTY. I gave up on dignity *years* ago. I am prolific. That's my revenge. If you want dignity you should marry a lighting designer.

OTTOLINE. Perhaps now we have worn out our terror, or at least winded it.

HAUTFLOTE. At darkest midnight December in the bleak mid-winter athwart the crest of Abel's Hill on Martha's Vineyard six moderately inebriated playwrights stood shovels poised to inter...

FLATTY. Illegally.

HAUTFLOTE. ... the earthy remains of a seventh.

HAPPY. Who might at least have agreed to the convenience of a cremation.

HAUTFLOTE. Being a creature of paper as well as of the fleeting moment Ding naturally had a horror of fire. *I knew him best.* For a long time now. I loved him.

OTTOLINE. We all did.

HAUTFLOTE. Yet not one of us dares break ground.

HAPPY. Wind perhaps, but never ground.

ASPERA. Wind for sure but not the Law. But is it the law or what's underground which immobilizes us? Incarceration or an excess of freedom? Enchainment or liberation? For who knows what dreams may come? Who knows what's underneath? Who knows if anything is, if the shovel will strike stone, or pay dirt, or nothing whatsoever?

BIFF. It's the Nothing stopping me. I can speak only for myself.

FLATTY. Bad thing in a playwright.

BIFF. The Horseleech hath two daughters. There's a play in there, somewhere, of course, I used to say: it won't come out. Fecal or something, expulsive metaphor. I was stuffed, full and withholding.

In more generous times. Before the fear... of the Deficit, before the Balanced Budget became the final face of the Angel of the Apocalypse. Now instead I say: I'm not going to go there. A geographical metaphor. Why? *I'm nearly forty* is one explanation. *"There"* meaning... That bleachy bone land. Into the pit. That plot. To meet that deadline.

OTTOLINE. When is the play actually due?

BIFF. Day after yesterday.

HAPPY. Rehearsals starting...?

BIFF. Start*ed*.

ASPERA. What, without a script?

BIFF. They're *improvising*.

(Everyone shudders.)

FLATTY. You shouldn't be here! You should be home writing!

BIFF. Did I mention how much I hate you, Flatty.

FLATTY. Marry a lighting designer. It worked for me. Sobered me right up.

HAPPY. I never meant... This reverse transcription thing. I'll work on it.

ASPERA. You do that.

HAPPY. I never meant to equate Hebrew and... It's just the words: reverse transcription. *Thinking* about it. Something I can't help doing. Writing began with the effort to record speech. All writing is an attempt to fix intangibles—thought, speech, what the eye observes—fixed on clay tablets, in stone, on paper. Writers *capture*. We playwrights on the other hand write or rather "wright" to set these free again. Not inscribing, not *de*-scribing but... *ex*-scribing(?)... "W-R-I-G-H-T," that archaism, because it's something earlier we do, cruder, something one does with one's mitts. One's paws. To claw words up...!

(HAPPY falls to his knees beside DING, and starts to dig with his hands.)

HAPPY. To startle words back into the air again, to... evanesce. It is... unwriting, to do it is to die, yes, but. A lively form of doom.

ASPERA. Ah, so now you are equating...

HAPPY. It's not about *equation*. It's about the transmutation of horror into meaning.

ASPERA. And doomed to fail.

HAPPY. Dirty work...

(HAPPY shows his hands.)

ASPERA. A mongrel business. This Un-earthing.

HAUTFLOTE. For which we Un-earthly are singularly fit. Now or never.

BIFF. I'm nearly forty. My back hurts.

FLATTY. Whose doesn't? No dignity but in our labors.

(THEY hoist their shovels.)

ASPERA. Good night old Ding. Rest easy baby. And flights of self-dramatizing hypochondriacal hypersensitive self-pitying paroxysmical angels saddlebag you off to sleep.

BIFF. *(Apostrophizing DING's corpse.)* Oh Dog Weary.

HAUTFLOTE. Many of these graves are cenotaphs, you know. Empty tombs, honorifics. Sailors lost on whalers, lost at sea, no body ever found, air and memory interred instead. All other headstones in the graveyard peristalithic to these few empty tombs, whose ghostly drama utterly overwhelms The Real.

OTTOLINE. Dig. Shovel tips to earth. *(They are.)* The smell of earth will rise to meet us. Our nostrils fill with dark brown, roots ends, decomposing warmth and manufactory, earthworm action. The loam.

FLATTY. I don't want to go to jail. Doesn't David Mamet live around here somewhere?

OTTOLINE. Push in.

(THEY do.)

THE END

WATERBABIES

by

ADAM LeFEVRE

WATERBABIES
by **Adam LeFevre**

Directed by **Simon Ha**

Emma.. ....Kate Goehring
Liz ....Jennifer Hubbard

Scenic Designer **Paul Owen**
Costume Designer **Kevin R. McLeod**
Lighting Designer **Ed McCarthy**
Sound Designer **Martin R. Desjardins**
Properties Designer **Ron Riall**
Stage Manager **Juliet Horn**
Assistant Stage Manager **Andrew Scheer**
Dramaturg **Michael Bigelow Dixon**

WATERBABIES

(Lights Up. A small office in the newly constructed wing of a YMCA complex in a medium-sized American city. An institutional metal desk with chair, a small couch, a bookcase with a few books for and about children. On the wall, a big daisy made out of construction paper, each petal a different color, each bearing the name of a child—Becky, Andrew, Travis, etc.—and a painting, a seascape, perhaps a print of a Winslow Homer.)

(EMMA sits quietly on the couch. In her lap lies a swaddled little body. Enter LIZ, as if turning from one corridor into another. She holds a scrap of paper in her hand, referring to it as she talks to herself.)

LIZ. Right, down the third green hallway. That was the third green hallway. First blue door on the left. Whose left? God, I don't have a clue where I am. Blue door. *(She turns and sees EMMA.)* Oh! Hi. Water babies? Am I here?

EMMA. He's almost down.

LIZ. Uh oh. Nap time? Am I late?

EMMA. His eyes are open. I don't know.

LIZ. There was construction everywhere. Central Avenue closed entirely. The arterial backed up to Henshaw. Flashing arrows funneling traffic into one lane. Normally nice people, they get behind a wheel in a situation like that, presto!, swine. Total maniac piglets. And forgive me, this new wing, it's gorgeous, but it's not the *Y* I remember. These color-coded corridors, I cannot fathom.

EMMA. *(Speaking to her bundle.)* No, no. Shh.

LIZ. Ooops.

EMMA. Don't do this to me. It's my life now.

LIZ. I'll whisper.

EMMA. Don't worry. Once he's down, he sleeps like a... like a... lo... like a law... Damn! Like a lull...

LIZ. Is this a bad...

EMMA. Lobster! A lobster. He sleeps like a lobster. There. Bingo.

LIZ. Cause if this is a bad time...

EMMA. It's not good or bad, long as it floats.

LIZ. ... I could come back. No problem. I've got errands to do, and Jim, my husband Jim's got the baby at home. He takes Wednesday afternoons off now, which is such a blessing. A legitimate breather for me, and he gets his one-on-one Daddy time with Duncan. Am I talking too loud? How old's your little guy?

EMMA. He's... He's about... Oh God, I don't know. You know those days when everything...

LIZ. Boy, do I. I mean, having a kid...

EMMA. Everything is just so...

LIZ. Changes everything, doesn't it?

EMMA. Boneless. Unbraided. Blended in? Something with a *B* in it. *(To bundle.)* Lullabybye, Snookums. Sneepytime.

LIZ. What's his name?

EMMA. Oh God. Okay. It's... It's... Lo... Law... Lolaw...

LIZ. It's not important.

EMMA. It's his *name*, for Christsake! I'll get it.

LIZ. Why don't I come back?

EMMA. Blob! No! Bob! Bob. This is my boy, Bob. *(She gently tucks him under the chin.)* Bobby, blobby. Li'l puddin' face. Wow, he's really under now. I'm losing my ambivalence about the immediate future. What is it you want?

LIZ. I called you, remember? I have some questions about Water Babies.

EMMA. Oh, yes. Water Babies.

LIZ. Just some quick ones, you know, about the philosophy of the time-frame, you know. What's developmentally appropriate specifically *vis a vis* Duncan, who's pretty advanced, according to our Doctor, physically. It's amazing, really. He'll be eleven months next week, and he's *this* far from walking. Because I've read if you wait too long, with some kids—and unfortunately, we only just heard about your program from my friend, Diane, who, by the way, said you just had a *knack* with the little ones. *Enchantress*, in fact, was the word she used. Anyway, I read if you start too late it can be traumatic and actually instill a fear, you know, of the water and create an obstacle the child then later on down the road has to overcome. If you wait, that is. If you wait too long. Before you start. So, I was just concerned that at eleven months we may have missed the boat, so to speak, with Dunkie. But I don't know, of course. Because this is not... my area. So. *(A pause.)* I guess your Bobby's a water baby.

EMMA. It's in the blood.

LIZ. So, how old was he when he started?

EMMA. Oh God, here we go again. Okay, wait. I'll get it. Bob was... When we met he was already nearly this size, so that would make him... It's conceivable he was younger, by a breath or two. Maybe. But you know he's not really mine so none of this is written in stone.

LIZ. Oh. He's adopted.

EMMA. Listen. You hear that?

LIZ. No.

EMMA. He doesn't get that from me. Does your son speak?

LIZ. Oh, yes. Lots of words. Doggie. Horsey. Moomoo.

EMMA. Horsey and Moomoo. Wow. Think I should worry about Bob?

LIZ. No. I mean, well... *How* old is he? No. I mean, no. Each one is just different. Each has his or her own way. Like my sister-in-law's little boy, Wade. He didn't say a word till he was nearly three and a half years old. Then, all of a sudden, one morning, this torrent of language just poured forth from this child's mouth—all these words they had no idea where he'd even heard them, as if they'd been jammed up inside his little brain and finally on this particular day, the dam just burst.

EMMA. This morning I thought I heard him say *waffle*. But he was just choking.

LIZ. Dunkie says *waffo*. And *maypo suppo*.

EMMA. I had to give him a real smack on the back.

LIZ. He calls it *maypo suppo*.

EMMA. Calls what *maypo suppo?*

LIZ. Syrup. Maple syrup.

EMMA. Don't worry. He'll get it.

LIZ. I'm not worried.

EMMA. Bob doesn't talk. He kind of transmits. You gotta stay on your toes.

LIZ. Have you been doing this a long time?

EMMA. What?

LIZ. Teaching infants to swim.

EMMA. Oh. I've been involved in aquatic education all my life. When I was a kid, I tried to teach myself to breathe through my eyes. I just thought I could do it.

LIZ. Aw. That's cute.

EMMA. No, I was absolutely serious about it. I sensed inside me this skill, this ancient, lost skill which I was sure I could salvage from the deep of my memory. I practiced in the bathtub. Kept my mouth and nose just below the surface of the water, and concentrated on bringing air in through my tear ducts, and around my eyes. I never got it. Swallowed a lot of water too. But I learned... that the breath... cannot be contained. It must circulate, always and forever. And that I could not disappear... into what contained *me*... and remain... myself.

LIZ. Wow, so you've really developed a philosophy, haven't you. It's not just the doggypaddle and back-float any more.

EMMA. That brain is 80% water. Does that answer your question? That wasn't your question, was it. Damn. I'm sorry. What is it you want to know?

LIZ. Is Duncan too advanced for Water Babies? Jim is very gungho. I'm just... I may be a little over-protective, I guess. I just don't want anything bad to happen.

EMMA. Well, I don't know then. You see, it's like a dream. In a liquid environment, there are no guarantees.

LIZ. I mean, he's just a baby. I don't want him traumatized. I don't want him set back in any way. As a mother you know what I mean.

EMMA. No. No I don't. You think this is the Marines?

LIZ. No, of course not...

EMMA. Just what do you think I intend to do to little Dunkie?

LIZ. You misunderstand me.

EMMA. Roast him and eat him like a Peking Duck?

LIZ. No, please. I just...

EMMA. Lookit! Ol' Dunkie and me will get along just fine so long as he leaves the *moomoo doggie* out of it. We're swimmers here, not talkers.

LIZ. I'm not worried about *you*. I'm worried about the water.

EMMA. Oh, well. That's different. It is always wise to cast a cold and narrowed eye upon the water. Water can take you places from which, unless you're very careful, there is no return. Places so deep, so quiet, so beautiful, it's more than the human heart can bear. It's always good to pause at water's edge. Hesitation, as they say, is Wisdom's crippled child. For Duncan's sake, let's be perfectly quiet for a moment. No words in the world for awhile but water's words.

LIZ. I...

EMMA. Shh! *(There's a considerable pause. EMMA cocks her ear toward BOB.)* You hear that? Didn't that sound like *waffle*?

LIZ. I have to talk to Jim.

EMMA. How would he know?

LIZ. About Water Babies for Duncan. We just have to discuss it a little more before we can make an informed decision.

EMMA. That's a mistake. Men don't trust water. They can't fix it. It eludes them. Not their fault. Just the way it is. Jim'll steer you wrong on this, believe me. The hell with Jim is my advice. Though I'm sure he's an excellent man.

LIZ. We're a team. That's the way we do things. Sorry, I'll just have to get back to you when we decide what to do. Is it the same phone number?

EMMA. I should have told you. There's no space left in this session anyway. All filled up. Just before you arrived a baby crawled in here and formed a complete sentence. Crawled right up into my lap and said, you believe this, without a trace of a lisp or coo, said, "I shall test the deep." I mean, talk about *advanced*. I was just bowled over by the presence and self-possession of this little fry who couldn't have been more than a handful of moons old. So, I said, "Bless your soul, child, you're in! You're my last water baby." So, you see, there's just no room. Unless someone drops out. Or drowns.

LIZ. I'm sorry.

EMMA. Maybe next session.

LIZ. Maybe.

EMMA. Or maybe not. Your choice. I'm pro-choice. *(To BOB.)* Don't. Don't. Lullaby-bye. Lullaby-bye.

LIZ. He's waking up?

EMMA. Dreaming. I think he's dreaming. His eyes are open, but he looks very far away.

LIZ. Can I take a peek? I just adore babies.

EMMA. No. No!

LIZ. Okay. Is everything all right? Is your baby all right?

EMMA. Sometimes you have to listen with your feet to hear the S.O.S. from your heart. You don't understand, do you?

LIZ. I'm a mother. Like you. I just want my child to be healthy and happy and safe. That's why I came. That's why I wanted to talk to you. Because I thought you would be able to advise me.

EMMA. I did my best, my level best.

LIZ. Thanks for your time.

EMMA. It was nothing.

LIZ. I hope I can find my way out of here.

EMMA. Just keep turning as the colors change—blue to green, green to yellow, yellow to red, red to white. At the end of the white there's a big glass door. That's it. That's out.

LIZ. Thanks. Blue to green, *et cetera.* Thanks. Diane, my friend, she says you're an extraordinary teacher. She recommended you. I thought you might like to know.

EMMA. Diane? I don't remember. So many babies, so many mothers. It's hard. I've already started to forget you. It just goes on and on.

LIZ. Good-bye. Good luck with all your water babies.

(Exit LIZ.)

EMMA. *(She looks down at swaddled BOB.)* Luck. Luckabyebob. I remember it. Like an arrow. The first time I saw you. Flash of silver as you arced into the sunlight. The thrash sending white spray high over the gunnels into my bloodied sheets. Like being struck by an arrow. God. My heart stopped. Then it started beating backwards. I should've thrown you back. I should've thrown you back right then.

Now it's too late. I've been struck by your silence. I need to know your secrets. Talk to me. Stop dreaming. Bob? Bob? Say *waffle*. *Waffle*. Say it. Say *waffle*.

THE END

JUST ONE NIGHT

by

KIM LEVIN

JUST ONE NIGHT
by Kim Levin

Directed by Viatcheslav Stepnov
Dramaturg Jeffrey Ullom

Liz ....Heather LaFace
Kate ....Elizabeth Kay
Margaret ....Ana Mercedes Torres
Dave ....Adam Lang

Scenic Designer **Stephanie R. Gerckens**
Costume Designer **Kevin R. McLeod**
Lighting Designer **Kathleen Kronauer**
Sound Designer **Martin R. Desjardins**
Properties Designer **Mark Walston**
Stage Manager **Sarah Nicole Spearing**

CHARACTERS
Kate, Margaret and Liz: college students, early 20's, roommates
Dave, college student, early 20's

SETTING
An apartment on a college campus

JUST ONE NIGHT

(KATE and MARGARET are straightening up the apartment. LIZ sits on the couch, doing work. "Respect" is playing in the background.)

KATE. Will you get another bag out?

MARG. Sure. Do you know if there are any more under the sink?

LIZ. I just brought some more in yesterday, so there should be some.

MARG. God, I feel like I'm gonna heave. Last night was insanity.

KATE. I can't believe how many people ended up here after the Beta party. It's just a good thing we didn't get busted. I mean, we are only one warning away from being on social prob.

MARG. Well it was well worth the risk cause guess who came over last night?

KATE. Who?

MARG. Mac Templeton.

KATE. Oh, he is a bad man.

MARG. Honestly Kate, you say that about every guy.

(MARG turns up the music and she and KATE start dancing. LIZ is still on the couch working. They try to get LIZ up to dance, but she refuses. KATE turns the music back down.)

KATE. What's up with you woman?

LIZ. Nothing, I am just trying to work.

KATE. Are you OK?

LIZ. Yeah, I'm fine. I just have to get some stuff done. I have a make-up seminar tonight.

KATE. English?

LIZ. Yeah, it's my seminar on Friendship.

MARG. Well, did you have fun last night?

LIZ. It was fine.

MARG. I assumed you were having a good time since you got home so late and at the party I saw you and Dave talking alone in the corner for almost the whole time. I'm glad to see that you are finally doing something about your mutual attraction. So, did you hook? *(The phone rings.)* So?

LIZ. Go get the phone and then I'll tell you. It's probably for you anyway.

MARG. Alright, but I'll be right back.

(MARG goes out of the room to get the phone.)

KATE. Don't bullshit me Liz. I know when you are lying.

LIZ. I'm not lying.

KATE. Uh huh. So what's wrong? Is it Dave?

LIZ. Yeah.

KATE. What happened?

LIZ. Dave and I were hanging out together at the party and we were having a really good time. Around two when people started to clear out, I saw you guys with a bunch of people getting ready to go. I figured you were inviting people to come back and party late night, so I asked Dave if he wanted to go to our place. He said he was getting a little cold and wanted to stop by his room first to grab a sweatshirt. So we went to his room. While he was changing, I was looking through his CD collection. He had this great Neil Young import, so I asked him if I could hear it. So we were hanging out, listening to the CD and we started kissing and then fooling around.

KATE. And?

LIZ. I don't know, I just, I feel like, I don't know.

KATE. Did you have sex?

LIZ. Yeah.

KATE. Did you want to?

LIZ. No.

KATE. Oh, my God, I'm sorry.

LIZ. No, it's not what you think.

KATE. What do you mean?

LIZ. He didn't attack me or anything, I just...

KATE. Did you tell him that you didn't want to sleep with him?

LIZ. Yeah, well, yeah but...

KATE. But nothing Liz, he took advantage of you against your will.

LIZ. Just forget it Kate. I should not have even brought this up. I was just feeling a little weird about it and I thought maybe talking about it might help. I guess I was wrong.

(MARG enters.)

LIZ. Who was on the phone?

MARG. My Mom, she was calling to see when... what's going on?

LIZ. Nothing.

MARG. What's wrong?

KATE. Dave raped Liz last night.

MARG. Are you alright sweetheart? I mean, what happened?

LIZ. No, I'm fine. Kate is totally exaggerating. This is getting completely out of hand.

KATE. Oh, is it really?

MARG. What the hell is going on? Is this a joke? Will one of you please explain what's going on?

KATE. Well, since I have totally misinterpreted what happened to you Liz, why don't you go ahead and tell Margaret what did happen?

MARG. What?!

LIZ. I went over to Dave's room with him last night after the party. We hooked up and ended up having sex even though I really wasn't into it, alright.

MARG. What do you mean, you really weren't into it?

LIZ. First, we were just hanging out listening to a CD, we were on the couch talking and I leaned over and started to kiss him. I really wanted to, wanted to kiss him. He took off my sweater and started to kiss my neck. He was very gentle and sweet. Pretty soon we were both naked and getting into it. I was still having fun, but I knew I didn't want to have sex with him. He asked me if I wanted to and I told him that I didn't think it was a good idea. He asked me a few more times and I kept telling him no. I mean I tried to explain it to him, that it wasn't him but I just didn't want to yet. The next thing I knew he was on top of me and... I don't think he even realized what he was doing, that I didn't want to. I mean, I guess I had no business starting things. Oh I don't know.

MARG. I'm sorry that happened sweetie. I'm sure Dave didn't mean to hurt you though. He is one of our good friends. He would just die if he knew he upset you like this.

KATE. Give me a break. Ignorance is no defense. You're saying that because he didn't realize...

MARG. Kate, Dave is one of our best friends.

KATE. Oh, I suppose you're going to try to tell me that you can only be raped by a stranger.

LIZ. No that's not what she's saying. He got a little carried away. We had both been drinking and he just wasn't thinking.

KATE. A person under the influence of alcohol cannot legally give consent to engage in sexual intercourse. So it doesn't matter if you said yes or no, he still had no right to have sex with you.

MARG. Well that's ridiculous because that means that Dave could say that Liz raped him. Oh, I'm sorry. I'm just saying theoretically.

LIZ. That's beside the point, we had both been drinking and I should have known better than to put myself in that position.

KATE. I'm not saying that you shouldn't try to avoid bad situations, but that doesn't mean that you should take responsibility for what happened, that doesn't mean that Dave didn't do anything wrong.

MARG. Kate, they're both adults and both chose to go to Dave's room. I'm sure that both of them had a good idea that they would probably hook up and even further, I'm sure they both wanted to. I just think that if a person can't handle a situation then they shouldn't put themself in it.

KATE. Oh, I see, Liz couldn't control the situation so she just got what she deserved.

MARG. I am saying that people should take some responsibility for themselves.

LIZ. Will you all just stop!

MARG. We're just trying to help you figure this thing out.

LIZ. Well, thanks but you're really not helping. I was already upset and confused. I was lying in Dave's bed last night waiting for him to fall asleep. I think I was shaking. All I remember is that I kept thinking over and over, why did you have to mess things up, everything was going so well. His leg was on top of me, but I managed to get out of his room without waking him. I ran home and went straight to bed. I didn't want to think anymore. When I woke up this morning, I couldn't help feeling that it was my fault too, that I was somehow responsible.

KATE. Liz, listen to me, I understand how you feel, but don't let anyone try to make you believe that you are the evil temptress and that because you started things that you were responsible for seeing them through to Dave's desired ends. You told him that...

(Interrupted by a knock at the door.)

MARG. Are you alright?
LIZ. Yeah.
MARG. Come in.

(DAVE enters.)

DAVE. Hey!
MARG. Hey Dave, what's up?
DAVE. Nothing. I was riding my bike around, so I thought I'd stop by and see what you guys were up to.
KATE. Not much, we're just trying to clean this pit up a little after last night.
MARG. I'm gonna take this bag out.

(MARG exits.)

DAVE. Yeah, I heard you guys were raging last night.
KATE. It was pretty crazy.
DAVE. I'm sorry I didn't make it by, I guess I crashed pretty hard.
LIZ. It's okay. I was pretty tired too. Anyway I just came home and went to bed.
KATE. Liz, if you're looking for me I'm going to go next door and talk to Davis for a while, but I should be back in just a few minutes. See ya later, Dave.

(KATE exits.)

DAVE. Later, Kate. So what's up with you.

LIZ. Nothing, I guess I'm a little tired. I was having trouble sleeping last night. It was pretty loud here.

DAVE. I know what it's like, living in Division. I mean it gets so loud sometimes. It's a good thing that I'm such a sound sleeper, but it's almost impossible for me to study in my room.

LIZ. Yeah, I'm sure.

DAVE. When I woke up this morning and you weren't there, I was afraid something was wrong.

LIZ. No, I knew that I had a lot of work to do today, so I figured I should take off, so I wouldn't wake you up at the crack of dawn.

DAVE. I probably wouldn't have noticed. I just thought that maybe I was totally snoring and driving you crazy or that I was hogging the bed and pushing you off the edge or something.

LIZ. No, I was fine.

DAVE. Good. I had a really good time last night. You're the first girl, sorry woman, in a long time that I really feel that I get along with. God, I feel like a dork. I just wanted to to tell you that I had a good time.

LIZ. Thanks.

DAVE. Listen, I know that you have a lot of work tonight. So do I. But, I was thinking that maybe Tuesday night we could get some beer and hang out.

LIZ. Sure.

DAVE. Okay. Well, I'm gonna take off and let you do some work.

LIZ. Okay.

DAVE. See ya later.

LIZ. Bye. *(DAVE exits. LIZ picks up the phone and dials.)* Yes. Hello. This is Liz Phillips. I would like to report a rape.

THE END

COMPATIBLE

by

ANNA Li

COMPATIBLE
by **Anna Li**

Directed by **John Campbell Finnegan**
Dramaturg **Jeffrey Ullom**

Woman ....Linda Green
Man ....David A. Baecker

Scenic Designer **Stephanie R. Gerckens**
Costume Designer **Kevin R. McLeod**
Lighting Designer **Kathleen Kronauer**
Sound Designer **Martin R. Desjardins**
Properties Designer **Mark Walston**
Stage Manager **Sarah Nicole Spearing**

CHARACTERS

WOMAN
MAN

COMPATIBLE

(MAN is dressed in his finest pair of Italian pants and a truly beautiful shirt that goes so well with his lower half it is obvious he put thought into the act of clothing himself this evening. WOMAN is dressed the same. We are in the man's apartment in the middle of winter. The snow muffles the sounds of the city so all that is heard is the low volume of Earl Hooker's "Anna Lee." The two sit at a simple pine table upon which is a small platter of three caviars, a bowl of crackers, two flutes, and a bottle of Veuve Cliquot half gone. The apartment is decorated sparsely but with affection. The WOMAN is sitting on a chair, and the MAN is standing behind her, holding her jaw, while feeding her champagne in a kiss.)

WOMAN. I love you.
MAN. What? You what?
WOMAN. You heard me.
MAN. No I didn't. I did not hear you.
WOMAN. Yes you did. And you love me too.
MAN. What? I what?
WOMAN. You do. You love me.
MAN. How do you know I love you.
WOMAN. It's your birthday, which you didn't tell me. You bought me roses. You're serving me champagne and caviar. You're not answering your phone. You're not going out with your friends—you're not having dinner with your family. You said you wanted me here, you said this is how you wanted to spend your birthday. You must love me.

MAN. I thought we'd celebrate. All I did was buy some fish...
fetus... stuff. I'm never going to Macy's again.

WOMAN. Look, it's okay. I just want you to know that I know.

MAN. No—

WOMAN. —the way you look at me when you speak to me—

MAN. —oh no—

WOMAN. —the way you order food for us—Oh God we're an
Us—

MAN. —Oh My God—

WOMAN. Look don't be so upset. It's only love. It's not like a
disease.

MAN. YES. Yes it is like a disease. Just like a disease. That's
exactly it. I don't love you. I'm sorry but I don't.

WOMAN. You do. You call me. Before I call you. I have to return
your phone calls. You rub my feet at the end of the day. You buy me
flowers. You bring me frozen yogurt. You play me that song with my
name in it and your eyes smile at me. People's eyes don't do that
when they're disease-ridden.

MAN. Now wait a second—

WOMAN. Besides I like your life so much. You make your bed.
You do your own laundry and actually fold it. You own a full set of
dishes. You have backup toilet paper. It's unbelievable. There are no
mountains of pubic hair in the corners of your bathroom floor and
Oh my God YOU WIPE THE TOILET RIM. The first morning I
ever woke up in your bed you made me coffee with the perfect amount
of milk and sugar and I never even had to tell you how. We're com-
patible.

MAN. I don't know what to say. I don't want to hurt your feelings
but I just can't tell you that I feel the same way about you. I mean I
like you, I like spending time with you, but I am busy. You know, I
am a busy person. I have things to do all the time and I have lots of
friends to see and I just really can't afford to have a girlfriend right
now. *(Beat. Resentfully:)* Okay. Okay. I do think about you sometimes and you do make me smile, all right? And yes I laugh in my
dreams when you sleep in my bed and okay I think it's you when the
phone rings and Fine you feel like a feather in my arms and so maybe
I have never seen anything more beautiful than you in my bathtub—

WOMAN. I feel like a feather in your arms?

MAN. And to see you in my clothes in the morning is what I wake up for—

WOMAN. I make you laugh in your dreams?

(There is unbroken eye contact. The exchange is like a smooth over-lapping dance.)

MAN. And so what of it that you took my breath away the first time I saw you—

WOMAN. —the crowd melted away when our eyes met—

MAN. —and I will not forget until the day I die the color on your lips as they spoke to me—

WOMAN. All the sounds, the music, all the voices became you as you walked up to me and I watched your throat say to me, Hello, you must be—

(He takes her throat in his hand like a baby animal he wants to squeeze but not too hard.)

MAN. The feel of your delicate throat in my hands—

WOMAN. Your strong hands on my throat, claiming me...

MAN. I claim you—

WOMAN. ...demanding me...

MAN. I demand you.

(They kiss.)

MAN. Oh God...

(MAN gasps. His hands move to WOMAN's waist, he squeezes her flesh. They move to her thighs, wrap around the back of them, and he picks her up, leg by leg, so that they are wrapped around him. MAN's face is to the audience, so they see him clearly. WOMAN's face is buried in the crux his neck.)

MAN. *(Under his breath.)* I love you.

WOMAN. *(Hopping down.)* What?

MAN. What?

WOMAN. What did you say just right now?

MAN. What? Nothing.

WOMAN. You said I love you I heard you.

MAN. Well. Ah, no I. Uh, okay. No. I, I'm just not sure I. I haven't decided.

(Beat.)

WOMAN. You haven't decided? About me? *(Beat.)* Oh. Well. I didn't realize I was a choice. I didn't know you could do without me. I'll tell you what. I'll make this little decision easy. I'm going to go.

(She looks for her shoes.)

MAN. No don't. Just—please. Stay.

WOMAN. Don't touch me. This is not a game. This is my life. I am in trouble if I stay because right now you are not a choice for me. I've fallen in love with you. I'm twenty-seven and out-of-my-mind in love with you. Do you know what that means? This is not high school. I look at you and see dinners at home and planning vacations and the Sunday Times. I think you would be the most incredible father in the history of the world. And so maybe if we don't feel the same way about each other now we might not ever and I could not live through you loving me less.

MAN. You frighten me.

WOMAN. Fuck you.

(She starts to leave. He stops her.)

MAN. You make my head spin so fast I can't see straight. And I can't have that. Everything about you makes me suffer. I want to touch you so bad I hurt. The way you smell. My chest feels like it's burning when I'm with you and my eyes see you through store windows and I can't concentrate at work. I get nothing done anymore. Before I met you I had my own thoughts and my own feelings and I was in control and I never cried in movies. Now I come home and I sit in this chair and remember the things you say to me. I just want to sit and remember until the next time I see you. I'm like a fucking vegetable without you. One day you are going to die and then I will be without you. And on that day I will become nothing — there will just be all this pain—so I would like to avoid all that. If you aren't mine now then I won't have to lose you later. I won't have to break up with you, I will never have to fight with you, you will never sleep with another man, you will never die.

(Beat.)

    WOMAN. I love you.
    MAN. I was happy before I met you.
    WOMAN. Do you want me to go or do you want me to stay?
    MAN. I am just not ready to face the rest of my life right now. I think sometimes: Our children would have the most beautiful eyes, and then I start to hyperventilate.
    WOMAN. Does this mean you want me to stay?
    MAN. I'm so scared.

(She kisses him softly on his lips, then his cheeks, eyelids, ears, neck, head, nose. She pulls away and looks at him.)

    MAN. Yes. Please.

(He kisses her and lifts her up into his arms and then sits on the couch with her in his lap, kissing. Lights fade.)

THE END

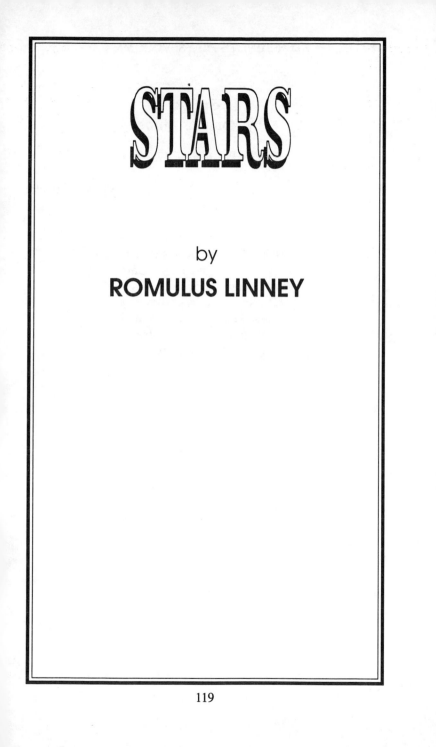

STARS

by

ROMULUS LINNEY

STARS
by **Romulus Linney**

Directed by **Frazier W. Marsh**

He.. William McNulty
She ....Karen Grassle

Scenic Designer **Paul Owen**
Costume Designer **Kevin R. McLeod**
Lighting Designer **Ed McCarthy**
Sound Designer **Martin R. Desjardins**
Properties Designer **Ron Riall**
Stage Manager **Chris Lomaka**
Assistant Stage Manager **Andrew Scheer**
Dramaturg **Liz Engelman**

CHARACTERS

HE
SHE

PLACE:
Manhattan

TIME:
The present

STARS

(A penthouse terrace. A summer night. Stars. HE and SHE, drinking wine.)

SHE. Stars.
HE. Great penthouse.
SHE. Like the party?
HE. Very much.
SHE. Like me?
HE. Very much.

(Pause.)

SHE. When people. *(Pause.)* What I mean is. *(Pause.)* Do you think suicide is more anger or sorrow?

HE. I have heard both.

SHE. I met a man named Norwood in Southampton at a club called The Dunes. It went out of business but that was the afternoon it opened, and my husband and I came from a rental on Shelter Island to a party in the bar and he left me there.

HE. What for?

SHE. My husband is very effective.

HE. I know that. You know I know that.

SHE. Drink, kiss. "Enjoy yourself." Off talking to a client.

HE. He's very effective.

SHE. So there I was. Five o'clock Saturday afternoon, Hamptons, smiling and bored. Norwood Struther wore a blue linen blazer, a red and yellow tie, silly and snappy. He didn't say a word. Men liked

121

him, slapped him on the back, called him Squeaky, kidded him about being a bachelor, fondly, but with some kind of something else about it. I couldn't tell what. Well, I was so sick and frustrated with my husband, mad at the world and my utterly asinine position that summer in the Hamptons, hello, there, Norwood, you squeaky bachelor, how are you, say something, and he did. He did have this stutter and high weird voice. I was desperate. I said, "Norwood, take me home", and he said, "All right." "Bartender, tell my husband I've gone to the movies." I was in Squeaky's bedroom in half and hour. He lived right on the beach, million dollar real estate Bridgehampton. Bedroom whole side wall open to the sea. God. God, you could hear the surf roaring and pounding. Wonderful. Kissing, hugging. He undressed me. Grand. But it took him awhile to undress himself. It took me awhile to notice it, then to see that he was choking, face red as a lobster, mortified, in that ravishing home, in our beautiful bed by the sounding sea. It was like he had an invisible collar around his neck, choking him to death. He had a very small sexual organ. Tiny.

HE. Oh.

SHE. He tried to apologize. I kissed him and said stop, it didn't matter.

HE. Did it?

SHE. Of course. He wouldn't talk to me afterwards. Mumbled something about reality I couldn't understand, stuck his head under a pillow, like a little boy. I had betrayed my husband—again—this time with a poor wretch lying next to me in abject misery. Outside on the beach, we could hear the surf pounding. The sea, powerful and potent, alive with cruelty and beauty. There was even moonlight, gorgeous, ravishing, and me and Norwood in that bed.

HE. By the sounding sea.

SHE. And my husband, who hoped I liked the movie.

HE. What does this have to do with suicide?

SHE. Look at the moon.

HE. All right. *(Pause.)* I'm in a bar on Columbus Avenue. I meet a woman who says she's a schoolteacher. We have fun, a really good time. She takes me home. It's good. I leave about eleven, she's looking at me like I'm an angel from heaven. Four o'clock in the morning, my telephone rings. It's her, sounding terrible. Help! Right now! So I go back to her apartment and she is looking at me like I'm a demon from hell. "What's the matter?" I said. "Did you call me on the phone?" she said. "When?" "Right after you went home." "No." "You swear?" "I swear." "Oh, my God, my God!" "What happened?" "What a fool I am! What a *fool* I am!" "*What happened?*" "Well," she said, "about eleven o'clock a man whose voice sounded I thought just like yours called me. You, I thought it was you, said you had a way of making us both some money right now but you needed two hundred dollars first, and I didn't have any cash, did I? Yes. Would I lend it to you. Oh, I had such a good time with you, I liked you so much, so I said yes, I have that, come get it. You said, no, you wanted me to meet a man and give it to him, with whatever else he asked for." "What?" I said. "You told me to go to a children's playground off Central Park West at midnight, and just sit in a swing and wait. You hoped I would do this for you. I was speechless, and God help me, I was excited. I got the money and went. There were shadows of people at the playground, coming and going in the darkness, there for sex. I was frightened and disgusted with myself and terribly, terribly alive. He was wearing a cowboy hat. When he came up to me and when I saw it wasn't you, I was horrified and thrilled. I gave him two hundred dollars and he pulled on his belt and I knelt down and gave him sex. He thanked me and was gone, leaving me there on my knees. I felt—well—debased but delivered. Then I thought, was that really like you? What if it wasn't you who called me? Was it? Oh, tell me the truth! We did meet in a bar but you were decent, weren't you? You wouldn't do that to me, would you? But who else could have? Nobody knew about us. It has to be you! "No it doesn't," I said. "It could be somebody in the bar." "Oh," she said. "But I don't go there often. I don't!" "Sometimes?" "Well, yes." She thought a minute. That man, with the cowboy hat, he could have heard us, heard I was taking you home." "Right." "But that means it was somebody who knows me, my phone number, and everything." "That's the only other possibility." "Oh, God," she said. "I don't know what to believe. Was it some man who's been watching me in that bar? Or was it you? Who did that to me?"

SHE. Do you expect me to believe this?

HE. It's true.

SHE. *Was* it you? You sent some man to do that to her for two hundred dollars? Which he kicked back to you?

HE. No.

SHE. Then who was it?

HE. I never knew. If she does, I never did.

SHE. It was you.

HE. Probably. But it wasn't.

SHE. I believe it was.

(Pause.)

HE. Did you keep up with Norwood?

SHE. I read about him, in a Long Island newspaper, two years later. In that beach house, with majestic surf and the ravishing moonlight, with two big pistols, one at each side of his head, both at once. Paper said there was nothing left of his head but the top of his neck.

HE. Point of the conversation.

SHE. Yes.

HE. Two years later?

SHE. About.

HE. It was the day after.

SHE. A week.

HE. A day.

SHE. A day.

HE. I steal her money. You laugh at him. Point of the conversation?

SHE. Did she die?

HE. Oh, no.

SHE. You saw her again?

HE. We married.

SHE. Still?

HE. Still.

SHE. You told me that awful story about your wife?

HE. She's in there now.

SHE. You're not going home with me?

HE. Not tonight.

SHE. Do you like your wife?

HE. Very much.

SHE. Then why are you here?

HE. Why are you?

SHE. I wish I knew.

HE. The moon.
SHE. Those stars. I'm shaking.
HE. I don't feel very good either.
SHE. I'm really upset.
HE. So am I.

(Pause.)

SHE. 858-5492
HE. 858-5492.
SHE. Mornings.
HE. OK.
SHE. OK.
HE. Stars.
SHE. Bright.
HE. Hard.
SHE. Cold.
HE. Still.
SHE. They never change.
HE. They never will.

(HE holds out his hand to her. SHE takes it, presses it, gets up and leaves. HE looks at the stars and shivers.)

THE END

WHAT I MEANT WAS

by
CRAIG LUCAS

For Connie Weinstock

" ... but he would have us remember most of all
     to be enthusiastic over the night,
         not only for the sense of wonder
         it alone has to offer, but also

     because it needs our love."

   —W.H. Auden, "In Memory of Sigmund Freud"

WHAT I MEANT WAS
by Craig Lucas

Directed by **Jon Jory**

Fritzie ....Allen Jeffrey Rein
J. Fred ....Bob Burrus
Helen ....Peggy Cowles
Nana ....Adale O'Brien

Scenic Designer **Paul Owen**
Costume Designer **Kevin R. McLeod**
Lighting Designer **T.J. Gerckens**
Sound Designer **Martin R. Desjardins**
Properties Master **Ron Riall**
Stage Manager **Carey Upton**
Dramaturg **Liz Engelman**
New York Casting Arrangements **Laura Richin Casting**

CHARACTERS
HELEN, 49
J. FRED, her husband, 47
FRITZIE, their son, 17
NANA, Helen's mother, 77

PLACE
A dinner table in Columbia, Maryland, 1968

WHAT I MEANT WAS

(HELEN, J. FRED, NANA and FRITZIE are at the dinner table in their suburban kitchen. All but FRITZIE are frozen, reaching for plates, mid-conversation. FRITZIE looks front; he wears jeans and a flannel shirt, untucked.)

FRITZIE. It's 1968 and we're at the dinner table in Columbia, Maryland—about 18 miles southwest of downtown Baltimore. Upstairs on my parents' dresser is a photograph inscribed to me from J. Edgar Hoover the year I was born. My mother has gone over the faded ink with a ballpoint pen so you can be sure to still read it. On this wall in another eight years will hang a letter to my mother from Gerald Ford thanking her for her letter of support. Right now we're in the middle of discussing the length of my hair and the clothes I have taken to wearing. The year before this I painted my entire bedroom black. Here then is everything we meant to say.

(The others unfreeze; they calmly eat their food and affectionately address one another throughout.)

J. FRED. What I think is probably at the root of our discomfort with your favoring long hair and denim is that for your mother and me and also for Nana, because we all survived the Great Depression and in some way feel we triumphed over that—coming from the working class and from immigrant stock, and because so much effort went into that struggle...

FRITZIE. Yes.

J. FRED. ... and we know in a way that you probably never will know what it means to go hungry and to have to work with your hands...

FRITZIE. Probably not.

HELEN. Let's hope not.

J. FRED. ... it seems an affront to our values to see you purposely dressing like a hobo. For that's what denim is, the costume of laborers, the unemployed. When we have seen so many people forced into that position very much against their will.

FRITZIE. I can understand that.

HELEN. And for dad's generation and mine, the idea of protesting a war which our own government has deemed to be necessary, much less desecrating our flag or burning your draft card, again flies in the face of so much we consider essential to our being.

FRITZIE. Yes.

HELEN. I know that a time will come when we will all look back and we'll say, "Perhaps this war was ill-advised," and, "Wasn't that quaint that we were so upset about the way Fritzie dressed," and we will recognize that we were probably as upset about the fact that you were growing up and we were going to have to let you go as we were about your hair which, in the final analysis, is absurdly superficial.

J. FRED. Yes, and your mother and I were also trying to grapple, in admittedly inchoate fashion, with the subterranean knowledge that you were, and are, homosexual.

FRITZIE. I know.

HELEN. And we didn't want you to live a lonely, persecuted existence which, after all, is all we were ever told about the lives of gay people.

FRITZIE. And I know, Dad, that I most likely made you feel in some way personally culpable, as if my sexual orientation were some cruel whim of fate, implicitly criticizing you for having been a special agent for the F.B.I. which did so much to help contribute to our national perception of gays as threats to society.

J. FRED. Of course, I can see now with the benefit of hindsight and the education which you have so patiently provided, that my activities in the bureau, though they may have added further burden to the lives of many gays already freighted with discriminatory law and at least one whole millennium worth of religious persecution didn't actually make you gay.

FRITZIE. No.

NANA. But you know, what I notice in all of this: Fritzie is struggling with the normal tensions and fears any adolescent would be having, regardless of his sexual orientation.

FRITZIE. Thank you, Nana.

NANA. And he is also trying, since he knows he was adopted, and now also knows that he was an abandoned baby—*(To HELEN.)* And though you didn't tell him that until you felt he could assimilate the knowledge in a way that wouldn't be destructive to his sense of self-worth.

FRITZIE. And I appreciate that.

NANA. Still Fritzie is searching for an identity, and that can't be a simple matter in a family which in many ways has hidden its own identity, and even fled from its roots.

HELEN. *(To NANA.)* Yes, by converting from Judaism to Christianity, you were effectively deracinating all your offspring and their progeny as well.

FRITZIE. But I can understand why Nana wanted to do that. Growing up Jewish in the deep South at the beginning of this century can't have been easy for her; and then the subsequent scorn heaped upon her by her sisters for what they considered to be her cowardice.

HELEN. And you know Nana's brother was homosexual.

NANA. Well, we didn't call it that; we didn't call it anything back then.

HELEN. When I married your father, Uncle Julian told me he thought your dad was "gorgeous." I was terribly embarrassed, and I wish to this day I could take it back and hug him and tell him that we loved him, no matter how he made love.

NANA. But I think we've made it difficult and confusing for Fritzie times—and at this very table—by referring to some of my relatives as "kikes."

FRITZIE. I guess it was hard for me to understand where all this animosity towards the Jews was coming from, especially from you, dad, because you weren't hiding anything; none of your relatives are Jewish, are they?

J. FRED. No, but you know how illiterate and ignorant my mother was. Well, you didn't really.

HELEN. No, I made your father ashamed of her, because I was; she was so uneducated, uncultured. Perhaps dad thought he could distance himself from the Jew he knew I was by—

J. FRED. My mother didn't want me to marry your mom.

NANA. I had called her up and told her we were Jewish. *(To HELEN.)* Because I didn't want to lose you. I didn't think I should be alone.

FRITZIE. *(To J. FRED.)* Mom's having ovarian cancer and the burden of keeping that secret from her and from me when I was eleven must have fueled some of your anger as well. You must have wondered how you were going to manage if she died, and been looking for someplace to vent that rage and fear.

J. FRED. Yes, I think I was.

FRITZIE. I can't even imagine what that was like for you.

HELEN. You know, I think in a sense I must have known it was true. That I was sick. Because the doctor wouldn't give me any hormones, and sex was so incredibly painful. I begged him. *(To J. FRED.)* I thought if I didn't give you sex, you might leave me.

FRITZIE. Maybe that's another reason why you and daddy drank so much.

HELEN. Well, Nana drank. And my father.

NANA. *(To FRITZIE.)* Everyone. And you will, too. And take LSD and snort cocaine. And risk your life by having sex with hundreds of strangers in the dark on the broken-down and abandoned piers of New York, even after the AIDS epidemic begins. You watched us losing ourselves over cocktails and cigarettes and thought, "That what adults do." You wanted to justify our actions, make us good somehow, by emulating us.

FRITZIE. I think all that's true. And Mom, I want you to know understand that the only reason you wanted to sleep with me and would crawl into my bed until the day I left for B.U. and snuggle against me and kiss me and breathe your liquory breath so close my face was that you yourself were molested by your dad.

HELEN. I was.

J. FRED. We've all seen and survived terrible things.

FRITZIE. In some ways I feel, because so many of my friends have died now—

J. FRED. Well, your first lover.

HELEN. And your second.

NANA. And Tom is sick now, too.

FRITZIE. Well... I'm more prepared to face my own death than you'll be, Mom.

J. FRED. Well, we have thirty years before she gets lung cancer.

FRITZIE. But Nana already is senile. *(NANA nods.)* And all of us are alcoholics.

HELEN and J. FRED. Yes.

HELEN. Well, not Nana.

NANA. I'm not really. I wasn't.

(FRITZIE kisses NANA on the cheek.)

FRITZIE. You were the first person I really knew who died.

J. FRED. No. My mother was the first.

FRITZIE. Oh, that's right.

J. FRED. I think you didn't say you were sorry the night we told you she was dead because I never held you or told you I loved you, and you had no idea how to relate to me emotionally.

FRITZIE. I really didn't. I didn't know what I was supposed to say. When I saw you cry at her funeral, I couldn't imagine what was wrong with you. I thought you had a foot cramp. Literally. It was so shocking—that contortion seizing your face in the middle of your walk back from the casket.

J. FRED. I do love you.

FRITZIE. I love you.

J. FRED. And I forgive you for saying it to me so often when you know how uncomfortable it makes me feel.

HELEN. *(To J. FRED.)* And I forgive you for never saying it in fifty years of marriage. For saying "Phew!" which, if you recorded it and slowed it down, might sound like "I love you." "Phew!" "I love you!" but to ordinary human ears sounds like "Phew, I didn't have to say I love you!"

J. FRED. And I forgive you for not having children, for being afraid.

HELEN. And I forgive you for not magically knowing the doctors were wrong about my kidneys being too weak, and for not being able to take that fear away, or any of my fears, because you were in some ways more afraid than I.

NANA. I forgive you all for screaming at me when I couldn't remember anything. *(To HELEN.)* When I picked up the knife and tried to stab you.

HELEN. I understood.

NANA. And for putting me in a home.

FRITZIE. Mom, I'm sorry I threw the plate of pasta at you and called you a "Cunt."

HELEN. I'm sorry I said your therapy wasn't working.

FRITZIE. *(To J. Fred.)* I'm sorry I embarrassed you by doing the cha-cha in the outfield and being so disinterested in and poor at sports.

HELEN. *(To FRITZIE.)* I'm sorry we didn't let you know it would be okay if you turned out to be gay.

NANA. And an atheist.

J. FRED. And a Communist.

HELEN. And I'm sorry I told you your father hated homosexuals when it was me, and it was only fear and ignorance.

FRITZIE. *(To J. FRED.)* I'm sorry I asked if I could touch your penis the only time we ever took a shower together, when I was four. I know that freaked you out.

J. FRED. *(To HELEN.)* And I forgive you for getting lung cancer.

FRITZIE. I do, too.

NANA. I'll be dead by then. *(To FRITZIE.)* I forgive you for calling me a racist pig when I said Martin Luther King was an uppity nigger.

FRITZIE. It's the way you were raised. *(To HELEN.)* I forgive you for telling me that my career was more important than going to the hospital in Denver with Tom when he had AIDS-related TB and that was the only place he could get treatment, and for suggesting that I should let him go by himself.

HELEN. *(To FRITZIE.)* I forgive you for lighting the woods on fire. And for making me feel like such a failure as a mother up until and even including this very instant.

J. FRED. *(To FRITZIE.)* And I forgive you for what you and I both know you did once and I can't say, or you'll probably be sued.

FRITZIE. Thank you.

HELEN. *(To FRITZIE.)* And I forgive you for trying to kill yourself and leaving that awful, long note saying your father and I were "NOT TO BLAME" over and over. I forgive you for pretending you didn't know me when I walked into the wall of plate glass at your grade school and broke my nose.

FRITZIE. I forgive you for not being the parents I wanted—articulate and literate and calm.

HELEN. People who knew how to use words like "deracinate."

J. FRED. "Inchoate."

NANA. "Emulate."

J. FRED. I forgive you for being ashamed of us, for telling us that you were going to look for your natural parents; I forgive you for not finding them and being so horrified at whatever you found you had to come begging our forgiveness.

HELEN. I do, too. And for telling everyone that I pushed you onto the stage and saying to Deborah Norville and Bryant Gumbol that you were gay when I asked you not to. When I said I would lose all my friends if you did.

J. FRED. Well... it was important.

FRITZIE. And you didn't. Did you? Is that why you seem so alone now?

J. FRED. No.

FRITZIE. Did I do that?

(HELEN looks at him for a moment. She gently shakes her head.)

J. FRED. Love is the hardest thing in the universe. Isn't it?

(Pause.)

NANA. No.

(They stare, lost in contemplation. FRITZIE gently kisses each of his parents on the cheek.)

THE END

MAKING THE CALL

by

JANE MARTIN

MAKING THE CALL

(An apartment or condo. A woman in her late 20s or 30s has just cooked herself an evening meal which she is eating in her living room while she watches television. She is attractively dressed, and there is a campaign plastic boater hat beside her. There is a knock on the door. She starts for the door, stops and asks...)

ELIZABETH. Who is it?

PARKER. Agent Parker.

ELIZABETH. Excuse me.

PARKER. Agent Parker, Secret Service.

ELIZABETH. I'm terribly sorry, but I think I'm not understanding what you're saying.

PARKER. Officer Parker, ma'am. United States Government.

ELIZABETH. I don't mean to be silly about this, but it's nine o'clock at night and opening your door to men you don't know saying peculiar things you don't understand... well, no offense meant, but I just don't believe I'll do that.

PARKER. Ma'am, I understand your point of view on this, but I am a Secret Service agent... probably one of the five or six men in America you can trust, and I have a message for you from the President of the United States.

ELIZABETH. A message from the President of the United States?

PARKER. Yes ma'am.

(ELIZABETH stands for a moment and then goes to her phone and dials.)

ELIZABETH. Margaret? It's Liz. Honey, I'm sorry I'm calling so late, but I need to ask you something. Well, that's so sweet of you... listen, Margaret, you know when we were down at campaign head-quarters tonight... yes, it was exciting, it was thrilling... yes, I thought he was handsome... no, I haven't washed my hand either... Marga-ret... Margaret! I'm sorry. I'm a little... I don't know... jumpy. Honey, there is a man outside my door who claims to have a message for me from the President. Yes. Yes, that's what he says.

PARKER. Ms. Waldrop?

ELIZABETH. Yes, he's out there. Well, that's just it, I haven't let him in. Calm down, Margaret. Do you open your door after nine o'clock to men you don't know? *(She listens for quite a long time.)* Thank you, Margaret. *(She hangs up the phone. She sits indecisively and then walks to the door and starts dealing with the three locks. She has trouble.)* Damn it. *(She tries again. No luck.)* Shoot! Officer Parker, I don't seem to be able to get my door open. You see I have memorized the sequence of the locks, but if I start out incorrectly... well, I just get... in a terrible mess. *(She tries again and then kicks the door.)* Officer Parker, the best solution might just be for you to tell me the message through the door.

PARKER. I do not believe that would be the best solution, ma'am.

ELIZABETH. Well, I can't open the goddamn door! I'm sorry, this is all just... very surprising. *(She tries the lock.)* Everybody who knows me knows I am the world's worst... the *worst* at surprises but Officer Parker... your name is Parker, right?

PARKER. Yes ma'am, Parker, ma'am.

ELIZABETH. The fact remains, Officer Parker, *that I can't get this door open*!

PARKER. Ma'am?

ELIZABETH. What!?

PARKER. Ma'am, I am a highly trained professional, and if you will step back from your door I believe I can effect entry.

ELIZABETH. Wait. Wait a minute!

PARKER. Yes ma'am.

ELIZABETH. I don't want you to break down my door.

PARKER. No ma'am. A highly trained professional would use other means in this case, ma'am.

ELIZABETH. If you will excuse me, Officer Parker, I need to go in the other room and get my handgun so that if you come through that door you can show me some identification. I'm sure you can understand such a precaution.

PARKER. Do you have a permit for that handgun, ma'am?

ELIZABETH. I will show you my permit at the appropriate time.

PARKER. You should be aware that there are tens of thousands of handgun accidents in the home annually, ma'am.

ELIZABETH. And if you are not who you say you are, Officer Parker, you are going to be one of them. *(She goes. We hear the whirring of a battery operated drill of some kind. She returns with a pistol which she trains on the door. In a moment, it opens. He is dressed in a Secret Service suit and tie.)* Freeze.

PARKER. Ma'am, I am going to move my right hand to my inside left jacket pocket to retrieve my identification which I will then hold out for you to examine. I don't want you to mistake said movement for an aggressive gesture.

ELIZABETH. Well, you make said movement, Officer Parker, and I will respond appropriately. *(He does. He holds out his identification. She moves to it, keeping the gun trained on him. She reads.)* Oh my God, you are from the Secret Service.

PARKER. Yes ma'am.

ELIZABETH. Oh my God.

PARKER. Could you possibly point that gun toward the ceiling, ma'am? *(She does.)* Thank you very much.

(There is a pause.)

ELIZABETH. Can I get you some munchies?

PARKER. I think I will pass on that, ma'am.

ELIZABETH. *(Sitting.)* Oh my God.

PARKER. I am not going to ask you for that gun permit, ma'am.

ELIZABETH. Thank you.

PARKER. Speaking outside the parameters of the service, I believe very strongly in home defense, ma'am.

ELIZABETH. Oh good.

PARKER. I could help you with your shooting stance sometime though.

ELIZABETH. Really.

PARKER. I hope you won't view my offer as sexual harassment?

ELIZABETH. No. No, of course not. Would you care to sit down?

PARKER. I believe I'll remain standing, ma'am.

ELIZABETH. I hope you won't view my offer as sexual harassment?

PARKER. *(Pause.)* You are joking with me, are you not, ma'am?

ELIZABETH. I'm glad you can recognize it.

PARKER. *(Deadpan.)* I like a good joke. Now, if you will allow me to proceed?

ELIZABETH. My life is truly bizarre.

PARKER. Mine is pretty bizarre too, actually. That was in the nature of a personal comment.

ELIZABETH. Oh.

PARKER. I'll proceed.

ELIZABETH. Fine.

PARKER. You are Elizabeth Waldrop?

ELIZABETH. Yes.

PARKER. Social Security number 451 42 8285?

ELIZABETH. I cannot believe this. Sorry. Yes, that's my Social Security number.

PARKER. You were present at Democratic campaign headquarters this evening where you shook hands with President Matthew Carver in a reception line?

ELIZABETH. Yes.

PARKER. At which time you exchanged a few words with him about the color of your gown?

ELIZABETH. We settled on mauve. You don't mean I said something to offend the President?

PARKER. No ma'am.

ELIZABETH. Thank heaven.

PARKER. President Carver, Mrs. Waldrop, is downstairs in the limo.

ELIZABETH. *(Pointing.)* Downstairs here?

PARKER. Yes ma'am. The President asked me to come up and inquire of you whether you would consider it too late in the evening for him to join you for acts of a private and consensual nature?

ELIZABETH. Excuse me?

PARKER. Are you interested in sex with the President of the United States, ma'am?

ELIZABETH. *(Pause.)* Well, that's a question I've never asked myself.

PARKER. You can imagine that he's on a pretty tight schedule.

ELIZABETH. My experience has been that most men are.

PARKER. Another joke.

ELIZABETH. Sort of.

PARKER. You would be doing the country a big favor, ma'am. There's a lot of stress attached to his job. You could help him out. It might mean a lot in the Mideast.

ELIZABETH. Why me, Parker?

PARKER. He thinks you are very attractive, that you have wonderful color sense, and he found your handshake "nurturing."

(A pause. Suddenly ELIZABETH breaks out laughing. It builds. It is literally a fit of laughter.)

ELIZABETH. It's all right. Really, it's fine. I'm perfectly fine. *(She breaks out laughing again.)* Excuse me. I don't... I have no idea why I'm laughing. *(She laughs. He steps forward and touches her neck with an extended finger. She stops laughing immediately.)* What was that?

PARKER. A pressure point, ma'am.

ELIZABETH. *(Pause.)* Ah. We, you and I, we're talking quite seriously?

PARKER. The President is serious, ma'am.

ELIZABETH. Do you know what is astounding, Parker? *(He shakes his head.)* What is absolutely, mind-bogglingly amazing is that I am considering it, Parker. And I'm not even crazy about sex! He wants to come up?

PARKER. *(Checking his watch.)* Yes ma'am.

ELIZABETH. Do we have a time frame here?

PARKER. I don't do the scheduling, ma'am, but let's give it a ballpark ninety minutes.

ELIZABETH. I assume some of that would be talk?

PARKER. Ten minutes minimum, ma'am.

ELIZABETH. Oh good, we'd get to know each other!?

PARKER. I have spent hundreds of hours with two Presidents, ma'am, but I have never gotten to know them.

ELIZABETH. I assume you haven't spent your hours in the way you suggest I spend mine.

PARKER. It is not within my parameters to suggest, ma'am. I am only empowered to inquire.

ELIZABETH. Do you prefer to be called Mr. Parker, Officer Parker or simply Parker?

PARKER. My first name is Woodruff, but I dislike being called that intensely.

ELIZABETH. Well, we've eliminated that then.

PARKER. Actually I like to be called by my badge number.

ELIZABETH. Do you?

PARKER. 991 actually.

ELIZABETH. You want me to call you 991?

PARKER. It's more intimate than Woodruff while still acknowledging I am here in a professional capacity.

ELIZABETH. 991, the President has a very high profile wife. Should we take that into account?

PARKER. No.

ELIZABETH. Ah. We shouldn't feel badly about that?

PARKER. Feeling badly would be a reason not to do it. *If* you do it, it's beside the point.

ELIZABETH. Well put, 991.

PARKER. We are trained to think logically.

ELIZABETH. May I ask why the President needs to get laid?

PARKER. It gives him the confidence to make important decisions.

ELIZABETH. Are we actually having this conversation, 991?

PARKER. We are, yes ma'am.

ELIZABETH. Are you intimating that my... participation... would fall into the "Ask not what your country can do for you but what you can do for your country" category?

PARKER. We are not trained in intimation.

(ELIZABETH sits down and dials the phone.)

ELIZABETH. Hi, Margaret, it's Liz. Oh I'm sorry. Well, it's a... theoretical question. If the President wanted to sleep with you, would you do it? Margaret, don't answer until you've given it a moment's thought. It apparently helps him make the big decisions. *(A pause while she listens.)* Thanks. *(She hangs up.)* I think I would like to call you Woodruff.

PARKER. If it would make you feel better.

ELIZABETH. Woodruff, let's say the President came up here... that we said he could come up... what would... what would go on then?

PARKER. My supposition?

ELIZABETH. You're trained in supposition?

PARKER. Yes.

ELIZABETH. Suppose for me. Woodruff.

PARKER. He would be charming. He would take your hand in both of his. His handshake is... electable. He would nod to me, and I would move outside. He would chat about his day... it would seem to be incredibly flattering and rewarding to be with a President chatting about his day. He would make you laugh... probably with the story about the Albanian ambassador. Then he would tell you that several of his decisions today cost people in other nations their lives. His eyes would brim. Then he would tell you how beautiful he thought you were at campaign headquarters and how beauty always makes him feel he can go on. Then he would look rueful. Then he would get up as if to leave. He would stop. He would turn back and then, maintaining eye contact, he would drop his pants and ask if you would suck his dick.

ELIZABETH. *(A pause.)* Yuk.

PARKER. I think so too.

ELIZABETH. *(A pause.)* I'm not going to do that.

PARKER. I don't think you should.

ELIZABETH. Thank you, Woodruff.

PARKER. What I think you should do is this. *(He reaches into his other inside pocket and takes out a small device.)* This is called a wire. You should go in the bathroom and strap this on under your dress. Then I should ask the President to come up. You should go through the whole thing right up to the moment when he drops his pants, then you should scream and shout, "No, no!" At that point, I'll hustle him downstairs and we'll drive off. Later I'll come back and we'll listen to the wire to make sure it's recorded. Then we'll go on the talk shows and write a book and make millions of dollars.

ELIZABETH. *(A long pause.)* May I call you Woody?

PARKER. *(Taking off his dark glasses.)* If I can call you Liz.

ELIZABETH. If I did what you suggest, Woody, what would you call our behavior?

PARKER. Because it is something the country needs to know, I would call our behavior ethical.

ELIZABETH. And the fact we would get rich?

PARKER. I would call that "fallout."

(A pause.)

ELIZABETH. Woody, before I make this decision, I will need to make one phone call.

PARKER. Sure, Liz.

(He puts his dark glasses back on. ELIZABETH dials. She waits.)

ELIZABETH. Hi, Margaret... *(Looks at her watch.)* Yes, I know. Margaret, this is just a theoretical question...

(Lights out.)

THE END

THE SIN-EATER

by

DON NIGRO

THE SIN-EATER
by Don Nigro

Directed by **Simon Ha**
Dramaturg **Jenny Sandman**

Sin-Eater ....Tommy Schrider
Younger Sister ....Caitlin Miller
Elder Sister ....Missy Thomas

Scenic Designer **Tom Burch**
Costume Designer **Rebecca Trout**
Lighting Designer **Laura Wickman**
Sound Designer **Elizabeth Rhodes**
Properties Designer **Mark Walston**
Stage Manager **Charles M. Turner, III**
Assistant Stage Managers **Anna Drum, Heather Fields,
Daniel William Gregg**

CHARACTERS
The Sin-Eater, a ragged young man
The Elder Sister, dressed in black
The Younger Sister, dressed in white

SETTING
A room in a house in Wales in another time, and the shore by the mill race, downstage at the edge of the light. In the room is a bed and three wooden chairs.

Sin-Eater: a person who in former times in certain parts of Wales, Scotland and England would through a ritual devouring of food and drink take upon himself the sins of the deceased. The food was often placed on the chest of the corpse. After the meal had been devoured, the sin-eater was driven from the house amid a hail of thrown objects and execrations.

THE SIN-EATER

(Lights up on a bed and three wooden chairs on an otherwise dark stage. A small house in Wales in another time. The Elder sister stands at the foot of the bed, in quiet mourning. The Younger Sister lies still in the bed. The Sin-Eater, a poor young man, watches them.)

THE SIN-EATER. My job always. Mother was before me. Someone must do it, she said, and we have been chosen. It is a dark privilege only we can acknowledge, she said. Their contempt is our badge of honor. We are the closest, she said, to understanding the mystery of Christ on earth. Like him, we are the sin-eaters. Live in a shack at the edge of the village. Shunned by all until their time of need. Someone dies, then I am summoned. But this time it was a different thing. Oh, Jesus help me. This time it was a different matter entirely. They were two sisters, I had watched them since they were little girls, the elder dark and quiet, the younger bright and lively, and both so beautiful, their eyes and their hair, to see them walk down green paths in spring, at water's edge in summer, through red and gold woods in autumn, on ice in winter, oh, those two, always together, always so lovely, the elder quiet, watching, the younger laughing, teasing the boys. The elder now and then took pity on me, brought me food, left it at the gate for me, but the younger threw rocks and called me names and laughed. I loved the younger. I loved the spirit of life in her. It is true she ripped my heart out with her hands on all occasions, and made jokes at my expense, but still I loved her, and could think no harm of her. Then came word I was wanted at their house. I hoped at first it was another cruel joke, but no. The younger had died suddenly.

149

She lay dead now in her bed. I must come and do what only I could do. Oh, God, oh, God, this is a more exquisite punishment and torment than ever you have given me. To enter that house. I have dreamed of that house. In my dreams I have walked in that house, and come to that bed, and crept into it with my beloved. Now I must enter it and eat her sins from off her breast.

THE ELDER SISTER. Well, what are you gawking at? Come here, boy. What is wrong with you?

THE SIN-EATER. I'm sorry. I just—I'm sorry.

THE ELDER SISTER. You act as if you've never done this before.

THE SIN-EATER. I've done this many times.

THE ELDER SISTER. Then why do you hang back like a guilty dog? She is dead, boy. She can throw no more rocks at you now. Do you think to take your revenge upon her by refusing to eat her sins?

THE SIN-EATER. Revenge?

THE ELDER SISTER. I know that she was cruel to you, and did torment you. I am sorry for that. She meant no harm, I swear to you, she did not. She had such life in her, it must be bursting out in all directions. She had all the world in her. Every grief and joy, every love and hate—no, not hate, there was no hate in her, there was anger, and impatience, and perhaps now and then a cruel sense of humor, but she was gentle, and loving, all animals loved her, and all souls on earth, but you, perhaps. You must not blame her for being young and sometimes thoughtless. She was a good girl, and meant no evil.

THE SIN-EATER. I never blamed your sister. She was welcome to throw rocks at me. I took great pleasure knowing that she lived. I grieve for her as you do.

THE ELDER SISTER. That is a very Christian thing.

THE SIN-EATER. No.

THE ELDER SISTER. Watch over her while I get the food.

THE SIN-EATER. Yes. I will watch over her. (The ELDER SISTER looks at the corpse for a moment, then goes. He approaches the bed shyly.) Oh, God. She is still ungodly beautiful. Even in death she seems to live. I cannot bear to think of her sweet body rotting in the earth. Jesus, Jesus.

(He falls to his knees and rests his forehead against the foot of the bed.)

THE YOUNGER SISTER. *(Lying motionless on the bed.)* The problem is, I'm not dead. I mean, it would seem that I am dead, but the fact is, I can hear everything they say, I can hear the owls out my window, I can smell the flowers in my room, I have heard my sister sobbing over me, I felt her tenderly bathe my corpse, which was not at all an unpleasant sensation, except that I wanted to tell her I'm not dead, only I could not speak, I could not move, I could not even open my eyes, and yet my heart beats, slowly, slowly, but it beats, I want to scream at her that I am alive, but nothing comes out. It is some sort of epileptic fit, it must be, I remember our mother telling me once that our grandfather used to have these, that once he interrupted his own funeral by sitting up and announcing that he wanted some crackers. How can I let them know I'm alive? Perhaps I can pee. Let me try. Ooooo. Ooooo. Alas, nothing. Not a drop. If only I'd had that extra cup of tea before my unfortunate demise. Oh, dear. What if they bury me? What if they bury me? Hello. I'm in here. Please don't bury me. Oh, why can't they hear me? And what is that loathesome boy doing with his head at my feet? I wish he would keep away from my feet.

THE ELDER SISTER. *(Returning with a plate upon which are placed bread, cheese and wine.)* What are you doing?

THE SIN-EATER. Praying for her soul.

THE ELDER SISTER. It is not the job of the sin-eater to pray. It is the job of the sin-eater to eat the sins of the dead, and thus take them upon himself. Here is the food. *(She puts the plate on the Younger Sister's chest.)* Are you ready? You don't look well, boy.

THE SIN-EATER. I don't know if I can do this.

THE ELDER SISTER. Of course you can do this. Why couldn't you do this? This is what you do. This is how you make your living, such as it is. If you don't eat my sister's sins from off her breast, who will? You are the only sin-eater in the village. What is it? Do you want more money?

THE SIN-EATER. No, no, it isn't the money. It's her.

THE ELDER SISTER. What's wrong with her?

THE SIN-EATER. Nothing. Nothing is wrong with her.

THE YOUNGER SISTER. I'm not dead, that's what's wrong with me.

THE ELDER SISTER. Then do your work and be done with it. There is bread and cheese and wine. Do you need anything else?

THE YOUNGER SISTER. I'd like some crackers.

THE SIN-EATER. No. This will be fine.

THE ELDER SISTER. I will be just in the next room. Let me know when you're done.

THE SIN-EATER. Yes. I will.

THE ELDER SISTER. I still can't believe she's dead.

THE YOUNGER SISTER. Me neither.

THE ELDER SISTER. She looks so lovely there.

THE SIN-EATER. Yes.

THE ELDER SISTER. Well. I'll go then. Don't take forever.

THE YOUNGER SISTER. Don't go. Don't leave me alone with this revolting person. I'm not dead. I'm not dead. Look, I'm attempting to pee.

(The ELDER SISTER goes. The SIN-EATER looks at the body.)

THE SIN-EATER. So sweet she looks. So innocent.

THE YOUNGER SISTER. I'm not dead, you simpleton. Can't you tell I'm breathing, you great, foul-smelling ignoramus?

THE SIN-EATER. I must eat her sins now. I must eat her sins. This is the one thing I can do for her. This is the only act of love which is permitted of me. I will never love another. I have only loved her. I will only love her. She is all the world to me. And now she lies here dead before me on her bed.

THE YOUNGER SISTER. I'm alive, you jackass. You blockhead. You lip-diddling imbecile. Can't you see that I'm alive? Get this crap off my chest and get away from me. You smell like a small animal has died in your pants.

THE SIN-EATER. I'm not hungry.

THE YOUNGER SISTER. Well, I am. I'm starving to death. Could I have a piece of that cheese if you don't want it?

THE SIN-EATER. I am so unhappy, I cannot eat.

THE YOUNGER SISTER. I can eat. I can eat. Just give me a drink of wine, why don't you? Listen to me, bean head. Hello? Hello?

An important message for the village idiot. Your beloved is not yet ready for the maggot farm. Hello?

THE SIN-EATER. Oh, God. I am having evil thoughts. I am having evil thoughts.

THE YOUNGER SISTER. Uh oh. I don't like the sound of that.

THE SIN-EATER. I must resist these evil thoughts. But I have loved her for so long. And now, to be alone with her, here in her bedroom—

THE YOUNGER SISTER. Help. Somebody help. Necrophilia. Necrophilia.

THE SIN-EATER. I have dreamed so often of this moment. Except of course she was not dead. Sleeping, perhaps. Oh, I must kiss her. Just once, just once before they put her in the cold earth, I must kiss her perfect lips.

THE YOUNGER SISTER. He is not going to kiss me. He is not going to kiss me.

THE SIN-EATER. I am going to kiss her.

THE YOUNGER SISTER. He is going to kiss me. He is going to kiss me. Now I wish I really was dead. Oh, oh, this is disgusting. This is disgusting. This— (*The SIN-EATER very tenderly and reverently puts his lips to hers and kisses her, a long, long, very sensual kiss. Then he pulls back.*) Jesus, James and Mary.

THE SIN-EATER. Oh, God.

THE YOUNGER SISTER. Oh, God.

THE SIN-EATER. This is a terrible thing, what I've done. This is a terrible, terrible thing.

THE YOUNGER SISTER. A terrible thing. Do it again.

THE SIN-EATER. And what's even worse, I'm going to do it again.

THE YOUNGER SISTER. Oh, good, he's going to do it again. He's going to do it again.

(*He kisses her again, long, reverential, and very erotic. In the middle of this the ELDER SISTER returns, sees them.*)

THE ELDER SISTER. Just what the devil do you think you're doing?

THE SIN-EATER. (*Jumping away from the body.*) Ahhhh. Oh, I

was just, I was—it's part of the ritual, we—

THE ELDER SISTER. Get the hell away from my sister. You despicable, monstrous creature. Get away from her. Get out. Get out of here. Get out. *(She is pulling him away, beating and kicking him.)* Out. Get out. Vermin. Excrement.

THE SIN-EATER. But I love her. I love her.

THE ELDER SISTER. I will tell the men of the village, and they will tear you to pieces, you vicious, evil, filthy, filthy man. Get. Get out. Get out.

(She chases him away. He moves downstage and sits on the ground at the edge of the light, in despair.)

THE YOUNGER SISTER. *(Sitting up in bed.)* Oh, no, you mustn't be mean to him.

THE ELDER SISTER. Mean to him? I'll be mean to him if I please. Do you know what that son of a— *(She looks at the YOUNGER SISTER, sees her sitting up.)* AHHHHHHHHHHHHHHH.

THE YOUNGER SISTER. AHHHHHHH. Don't shriek at me like that. Do you want to kill me all over again?

THE ELDER SISTER. What is happening here? Am I going mad? Have you come back from the dead?

THE YOUNGER SISTER. I was sleeping. Don't you remember about Grandpa and the crackers? Which reminds me, God I'm hungry. What have we got to eat around here? *(Grabbing the plate with the SIN-EATER's food on it.)* Oh, this looks good.

(THE YOUNGER SISTER begins to eat.)

THE ELDER SISTER. I don't understand this. I don't understand this at all. We had already dug the hole in the back yard.

THE YOUNGER SISTER. Maybe we can plant some azaleas. Now, run and get me some more food. Hurry. And bring back the Sin-Eater.

THE ELDER SISTER. You don't want to see that wretched man. He tried to molest you while you were dead.

THE YOUNGER SISTER. *(Chomping on the bread.)* He kissed me. He brought me back to life. It was incredible. My toes are still tingling. Go and get him. I want to see him. Now. Or I might drop dead again.

THE ELDER SISTER. All right, all right.

(THE ELDER SISTER runs out.)

THE YOUNGER SISTER. *(Sitting on the bed and eating, yelling after her sister.)* DO WE HAVE ANY LAMB CHOPS?

THE SIN-EATER. I've kissed the dead lips of my beloved. Nothing else matters now. The men of the village will come and tear me to pieces. I don't mind. I would rather be dead with her. I think I will just lie down here in the water. Yes, I will just lie down here and remember her kiss and let the water creep up over my head.

(He lies down on the stage, as if lying back in water, and is still.)

THE YOUNGER SISTER. FOOD. I WANT MORE FOOD. AND WHAT THE HELL KIND OF CHEESE IS THIS? IT TASTES LIKE FUNGUS.

THE ELDER SISTER. *(Returning with a plate of food.)* This is all we have left in the house.

THE YOUNGER SISTER. Great. Where is my Sin-Eater? I want my Sin-Eater.

THE ELDER SISTER. Listen, dear. I have some bad news for you, but I hope it will not spoil your resurrection. The Sin-Eater has drowned himself in the mill race. They have laid his body out there on the shore.

THE YOUNGER SISTER. He's dead? The Sin-Eater is dead? Are you sure? Couldn't he be sleeping just as I was? Couldn't it be like Grandpa and the crackers? Maybe it's contagious.

THE ELDER SISTER. No, dear. I am sorry. He is drowned.

THE YOUNGER SISTER. Oh. Oh, no.

THE ELDER SISTER. Here. Have some more food.

THE YOUNGER SISTER. I have lost my appetite entirely. Why would he drown himself?

THE ELDER SISTER. It must have been guilt for kissing your corpse. He didn't know you only slept.

THE YOUNGER SISTER. Oh, poor boy. Poor lonely creature.

He never knew. He saved me and he never knew. And what about his sins? Who will eat his sins for him? There is no sin-eater to eat his sins. He has died with his sins upon him, and all the sins he has eaten, and there is no one to eat his sins. I must go to him.

THE ELDER SISTER. You're not strong enough. You've just got over being dead.

THE YOUNGER SISTER. I must go to him now. He needs me.

THE ELDER SISTER. What could he need you for? The man is dead.

THE YOUNGER SISTER. I must eat his sins.

THE ELDER SISTER. You cannot eat his sins. You'll be shunned as he was. They will throw stones at you and spit at you.

THE YOUNGER SISTER. I don't care. I don't care. I must eat his sins. Someone must eat his sins. He gave me life and I must eat his sins. *(She takes the new plate of food and goes to the edge of the light, where the SIN-EATER lies still.)* Hello. I've brought you some food. Here. *(She carefully puts the plate of food on his chest.)* I'm going to eat your sins now. I think it's only right. I don't care if they shun me, if they throw rocks and jeer at me and spit at me. You kissed me. You gave me life. I want to do this thing. This is what love is, I think. The eating of the other's sins. And yet I have no appetite. You are really quite beautiful, you know. *(Pause. She looks at him.)* Perhaps just one kiss first. Would that be all right? You would not mind, I think. Just one kiss before I eat your sins.

(She gets down on her knees, bends over him, and kisses him long and tenderly on the lips. The ELDER SISTER watches. The light fades on them and goes out.)

THE END

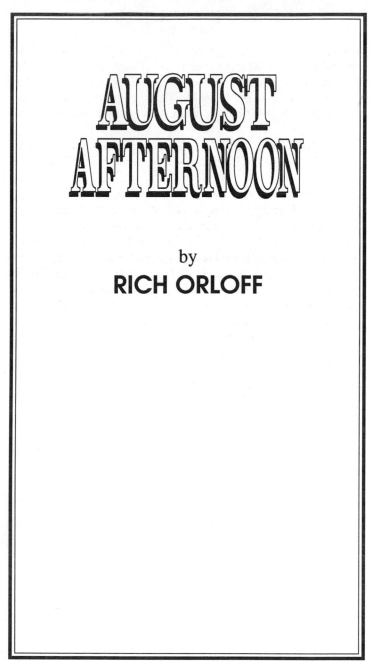

AUGUST AFTERNOON

by
RICH ORLOFF

AUGUST AFTERNOON

(The time is that period, earlier in the twentieth century, when cities were far apart, when men wore hats, when women never wore pants, and when everyone in America seemed to agree how people should act, even if they didn't always act that way in private.

It is late afternoon on a hot, sunny day.

The place is a motel room on a road outside of town. This is the kind of motel for people who don't expect much in their room. There's a bed, a dresser, and a single painting one would never look at unless stuck in a motel room.

There is a window on the side wall. Although the blind is pulled down, one can almost feel the hot sun trying to force its rays into the room. There is also a door to the outside—which should not be on the same wall as the window.

The people are the MAN and the WOMAN on the bed. The WOMAN, who has reached that age when young adulthood is becoming a memory, lies sideways on the bed, facing the wall. She wears a sundress which has been pushed up to her waist. Her panties and shoes are on the floor by the corner of the bed. The MAN, who is the same age, sits on the edge of the bed, leaning forward a bit, his hands resting on the insides of his legs. He wears a white shirt whose cuffs have been unbuttoned, plus a thin cotton undershirt, nicely pressed trousers, and socks. The man dresses to fit in, a goal he has admirably accomplished. His jacket and tie lay on the dresser nearby, and he has removed his shoes.

Also on the dresser is a pitcher with water and two glasses. On the bed is an opened book. It is a Bible.)

MAN. I'm sorry.

WOMAN. About what?

MAN. I—I just can't.

WOMAN. I see that.

MAN. It's not that I don't want to.

WOMAN. I see that, too.

MAN. I'm really sorry.

WOMAN. You don't need to be.

MAN. I didn't mean to... I shouldn't have... I've toyed with you.

(The WOMAN turns towards the MAN.)

WOMAN. Not as much as I hoped you would.

MAN. I led you on.

WOMAN. Everybody does that.

MAN. That doesn't make it right.

WOMAN. At least it got me out of the office for the afternoon.

MAN. You probably think I'm a fool, don't you?

WOMAN. No more than most men.

MAN. I'll take that as a compliment.

(The MAN picks up the Bible.)

WOMAN. I told you not to open that drawer.

MAN. I had to find a place for my—

WOMAN. You could've just put the damn thing in your pocket.

MAN. I didn't know this would be in there.

WOMAN. You don't know motel rooms very well, do you?

MAN. No.

WOMAN. Kiss me.

MAN. I...

WOMAN. Put the book down and kiss me.

MAN. I don't think that's a—

WOMAN. You won't fry in hell if you only kiss me. I promise.

(He's tempted, but...)

MAN. I, uh, I think we should go.

WOMAN. I'm not ready.

MAN. Pardon me?

WOMAN. I don't feel like leaving yet. It's too hot out. The sun'll melt me.

MAN. I think we should get dressed and go.

WOMAN. You can go if you want. I'm staying.

MAN. What will you do here by yourself?

WOMAN. I don't know. Read the Bible. Look for signs the Lord knows his ass from his elbow.

MAN. How will you get back to town?

WOMAN. I'll find a way.

MAN. Here, you can, you can call a—

(He reaches for his wallet. She puts her hand on his arm.)

WOMAN. Don't.

MAN. I didn't mean to—

WOMAN. I know. Just don't.

MAN. I can't just leave you here.

WOMAN. I bet you can.

MAN. Who do you think I am?

WOMAN. It's okay. I'm used to it.

MAN. Boy, you must've known some pretty awful men.

WOMAN. You know, I don't mind if you think I'm trash, but, but don't pity me.

MAN. I don't think you're trash.

WOMAN. And what *do* you think of me?

MAN. Well... I think you're pretty.

WOMAN. *(After a beat.)* Is that all?

MAN. No. Of course not. I, I like your hair.

WOMAN. *(Lightly.)* Men.

MAN. What'd I—

WOMAN. My Auntie Ro once told me, honey, beauty's only skin deep... and that's enough for most men.

MAN. I think you're a very nice person.

WOMAN. I think you're afraid to think otherwise.

MAN. I, I think we should go.

WOMAN. You can if you'd like. (*The MAN thinks for a moment and then starts putting on his shoes. As he starts to rise, the woman, who is seated behind him on the bed, lightly touches his shoulder.*) Please don't go.

(*She kisses his neck.*)

MAN. I, uh...

(*The MAN checks his watch. The WOMAN slowly puts her arm around the man.*)

WOMAN. The sun's making it so hot out there. It's as if God' suggesting we stay inside.

(*The MAN extricates himself from the WOMAN's arms.*)

MAN. I'm sorry.
WOMAN. There you go being sorry again. One would think you' gotten a degree in it.
MAN. Well, it's just, I—
WOMAN. Would you have actually felt sorrier if you had gon ahead and done it?
MAN. I'd like to think so.
WOMAN. What a world in which thoughts as those are our grea comforts.
MAN. I really should be going.
WOMAN. Stay a bit.
MAN. I really—
WOMAN. Please.
MAN. There's nothing going—
WOMAN. You can share with me your wisdom.
MAN. Well, I don't think *that'd* be worth staying around for.
WOMAN. Don't sell yourself short. I bet you can answer a que: tion I've never been able to figure out my entire life.
MAN. What's that?
WOMAN. How did you cure yourself... of yearning?
MAN. Pardon me?

WOMAN. How did you cure yourself of yearning? I know you yearn some, or you wouldn't be here now, would you?

MAN. Well—

WOMAN. You know, I bet I wanted to bring you here just to prove to myself that down deep, you yearn just as much as I do. I guess I was wrong. *(For a moment they look at each other and say nothing.)* So what's the secret?

MAN. Are you talking about lust?

WOMAN. Oh, no. No, no, no. It's been my experience that I can satisfy my lust much easier than I can ever satisfy my yearning.

WOMAN. Maybe you just haven't met the right man.

WOMAN. I don't think the right man would want me.

MAN. Now look, you're a very nice—

WOMAN. He might enjoy me, but he wouldn't want me. The men I've known, they begin to get real nervous when they find out how strongly I yearn.

MAN. I don't know what you're—

WOMAN. You see, I wake up yearning, and most days I go to sleep yearning. And when I look at other people, well, I just don't get it. It seems to me that either they don't yearn, or they've learned real well how to ignore their yearnings. But I can't do that. And I can't believe that the lives we have are the lives most of us yearn for.

MAN. Maybe you expect too much.

WOMAN. Once I tried to stop yearning. Cold turkey, like a drunk who decides to stop drinking. I said, "I'm going to go all day today and not yearn. And if I can do that, then I'll go for a week. And then a month." I made it through the day. And I got through the week. Never could make it through the month.

MAN. The Bible helps.

WOMAN. We must have different translations.

MAN. Maybe you need a dog. I have a friend who has this col-lie—

WOMAN. Maybe what I need is a different town. My mama, when she got old enough to leave town, she went straight to New York. And after a year of spending time with what she liked to refer to as " a vast array of cretins from around the world", she felt she had been cured of her yearnings. So she moved back home, read the Bible, and had a family. But she was wrong. She only *thought* she was cured.

MAN. I hear she lives in New Mexico now.

WOMAN. Yeah. Apparently she wanted to live someplace even hotter than this place.

MAN. At least it's not as humid.

WOMAN. You know, that year she lived in New York, she got a job as a manicurist in a nice barber shop. She told me men loved it when she held their hands. She said if she held their hands a long time, and was gentle with them, she'd always get a big tip. She told me, she told me that *her* mama had told her that men were only interested in one thing. But when she held their hands, she knew that wasn't true. But the problem was, you see the problem was that most men don't know that about themselves. And she always hoped that if one day she met a man who knew, maybe they could yearn together.

(The WOMAN reaches for one of the MAN's hands and holds it. The MAN lets her, but he doesn't participate. She lets go.)

MAN. I really am sorry if I caused you any... well, I'm just sorry.

WOMAN. You know, you feel sorry about as easily as I yearn.

MAN. Well, I, maybe I do, I don't know.

(The MAN starts to go. The WOMAN points to the drawer.)

WOMAN. You forgot.

MAN. Oh. Right... Thank you. *(The MAN opens the dresser drawer and takes out his wedding ring.)* She's really a very... special woman. She plays the piano beautifully.

WOMAN. See you in church.

MAN. Yeah. *(The MAN walks to the door. He looks at the WOMAN and starts reaching for his wallet.)* Are you sure I can't—

WOMAN. You know, when we were in high school, I didn't like you, but I always thought, there's one boy who's going to amount to something. *(She chuckles a moment.)* God, was I young. *(The MAN embarrassed, opens the door.)* I... I'm sorry.

MAN. Me, too.

(The MAN exits. The WOMAN sits on the bed. She gives herself a moment to take in what has happened that afternoon, and then she gives herself another moment to let go. She walks over to the window and raises the blind. Late afternoon sunlight, sharp and strong, shines into the room.

The woman retrieves her panties, but before she puts them back on, she stops. She feels the sunlight on her back. She turns around and faces the sun. She is in the middle of the sunlight coming through the window. She drops her panties. She removes her sundress. She pauses a moment and then takes off her bra. She breathes in the sunlight. She breathes it in deeper and starts to lightly caress herself. Her hands move up to her heart, as if guiding the sun's rays there. She takes a deep breath, letting the sunheated air fill her lungs with warmth.

She is serene. She gives herself completely to the sun.)

THE END

by

JOSÉ RIVERA

For Roberto Gutierrez Varea

187 was first workshopped in New York by Naked Angels, John McCormack, artistic director, as part of their Naked and Hate Free program, July 24, 1996. The play was directed by Charlie Stratton and featured the following cast:

Alejandra ....Camilia Sanes
John ....Gareth Williams

187
by José Rivera

Directed by **Jennifer Hubbard**
Dramaturg **Liz Engelman**

John ....Danny Seckel
Alejandra ....Monica Bueno

Scenic Designer **Tom Burch**
Costume Designer **Kevin R. McLeod**
Lighting Designer **Laura Wickman**
Sound Designer **Elizabeth Rhodes**
Properties Designer **Mark Walston**
Stage Manager **Charles M. Turner, III**
Assistant Stage Managers **Anna Drum, Heather Fields,
Daniel William Gregg**

(The City of Industry, CA. Present day. Five P.M.
A bus stop.

ALEJANDRA waits for a bus. She's exhausted after working an eight
    hour day in a factory. JOHN comes running up to her. He's run a
    long distance. He's exhausted from working the same job.)

JOHN. *(Out of breath.)* There's something I have to tell you...
ALEJANDRA. I'm sorry...
JOHN. ... hi... hi... I'm sorry, hi...
ALEJANDRA. ... I'm waiting for...
JOHN. *(Catching his breath.)* I—I don't chase people.
ALEJANDRA. ... the number eighteen bus...
JOHN. I have my pride, you know. Pride's very important these
days. Not much of it left. 'Specially when you're working a shit job
like we are, huh?
    ALEJANDRA. ... I think I see it coming! *Ay, gracias a Dios!*
    JOHN. The conditions in that place... like a slave labor camp...
some gulag... I don't think they're gonna pass a hike in the minimum
wage... looks like we're stuck in this Dickensian hell forever...

(The bus passes by. It's not the one ALEJANDRA is waiting for.)

    ALEJANDRA. No... *carajo*... it's the number six...
    JOHN. Dust, cat shit, bad lighting, noise, filth, low pay: it's im-
moral is what it is; but it's *work*, I guess, and I don't let the work get
me down. I have my pride, like I said. That's why I feel weird, you
know? Chasing you. I don't chase people.

(ALEJANDRA looks at JOHN for the first time.)

ALEJANDRA. You have your pride.

JOHN. *Exactly!* Yes! How did you know that?

ALEJANDRA. I have my pride too. I'm waiting for...

JOHN. The number eighteen bus.

ALEJANDRA. It's late! *Que mierda!*

JOHN. Hard to have a lotta pride when you're waiting for a bus, I imagine. *(Beat.)* I've got an old T-bird. Twenty trillion miles. But it's a shit kicker. Red interior. Original everything—except the engine. Which I rebuilt myself. You've probably seen it in the lot. It's right over...

ALEJANDRA. *(Turning to him.)* I don't want to talk to you.

JOHN. ... there. I could drive you... I mean, I swallowed my pride and ran all the way out here chasing you to ask if I could drive you home in my ancient but very cool T-bird. Wanna?

ALEJANDRA. No thank you. It's not personal, *pero yo no quiero ir contigo. Entiendes?* You see?

JOHN. Not really. I'm John.

ALEJANDRA. *(To herself.)* Ay Dios! Si este pendejo no me deja tranquila, me voy a poner a gritar!

JOHN. You're from a Spanish speaking country. But you don't look like a lot of the Spanish speakers at the plant. You are, uh... well... they're kinda smaller... they have more Indian, I guess, features... dark... and eyes that really penetrate... you don't know what their minds are doing... you look into their eyes and it's like looking into an infinite tunnel going into this deep ancient place and all you can see is this dark alphabet spelling words and feelings you can't read. You're not like them. *Your* eyes aren't so... unfathomable. There's light in that tunnel. A sparkle. Something I can recognize and read. A friendliness. Like you don't wanna, you know, cut me up on some Mayan pyramid and offer my heart to some jealous horrible god. You're not gonna do that! There's a frightening, primitive *distance* I feel with the other Spanish speakers at work. But you're different. You're a different branch of the Spanish speaking world. Where is your home? Where?

ALEJANDRA. *(Reluctant.)* Argentina.

JOHN. *(Smiles.)* That makes sense. There's something more Italian about you than those Guatemalan chicks I see all the time. A Sophia Loren kinda quality...

ALEJANDRA. What do you want? I don't want to ride in your car! Can't you tell that? I don't want to talk to you. How much more silent do I have to be to get you to go away? Do I have to slap your face? I'm not afraid of you. Some of the girls at work, maybe, are afraid to say something when they're harassed, but I am not. Is that what you want from me?

JOHN. Whoa, back up...

ALEJANDRA. You have no idea who I am. I am not Sophia Loren!

JOHN. I *know*...

ALEJANDRA. Do you know what I had to do to get here? Do you think there is anything you can do to frighten me? *Puerco! Cabron!*

JOHN. Just want to say hello. I don't know. You don't have to...

ALEJANDRA. I get up at five o'clock. I take two buses to get here, I work my... *como se dice*... my *ass* off for *no money*... and I take two buses to get home and you want to talk about my *sparkle*?!

JOHN. It's irresistible.

ALEJANDRA. *Idiota!*

JOHN. That didn't sound like a compliment!

ALEJANDRA. *Hijo de la puta madre!*

JOHN. I know what *that* is!

ALEJANDRA. Only a man could see through the sweat and filth in that building, the chemical smells, and the smell of rat poison, the dim lighting and monotony and cold and think of *sex.*

JOHN. A powerful drug.

ALEJANDRA. You don't know. North Americans don't know. There's an art to love. A culture of love. It needs the right conditions in order to live...

JOHN. I think it's got the right conditions right now.

ALEJANDRA. And I don't mean it can't be difficult. I know of people in prison who fall in love. People on their death beds. People without any other hope. And love finds its way to them and transforms them. I don't mean it has to be *easy*; but it does have to be *right*...

JOHN. Who's talking about love anyway? I just wanna drive you home in my car. I don't want you to wear yourself out taking four buses every day. I don't want to see you breaking your back any more than you have to. I'm offering you something good in your completely shitty day. I didn't imply anything else. You—*you*— brought up sex and love, not me!

ALEJANDRA. Then... excuse me. My mistake.

JOHN. I have feelings too. Latin Americans don't corner the market on feelings!

ALEJANDRA. But I did already say no to the ride and that's all I have to say about it.

(Short beat.)

JOHN. Yeah, that's fine. You can do that. You say no it's no. I'm not from the 1950s when no didn't mean jackshit to a man. I know what *"pendejo"* means: you can't call me that 'cause I ain't one! *(Slight beat.)* I was drawn to the light reflected in your eyes. It warms me. I don't get enough of that light in my life. Thought if you spent a little time in my car as I drove you home you could tell me about your world and I'd be able to enjoy that light a few extra minutes. *(Slight beat.)* Because I live in darkness. I live in a pit. I live among the moles and shrews and earthworms, all these eyeless creatures digging in the shit of the world looking for their love and their sex. You're the one person I've seen in a year in this city that's got more than survival on their minds, whose laughter I've heard louder and clearer than all the sounds of all the machinery in that fucking plant. I thought I could live on that a few extra minutes a day. To keep me from suffocating in the darkness. You have *that much* you could hold over me. That much. And I don't have anything. No money, no degrees, no family, no politics: just a pathetic old car my older brother gave me 'cause he felt sorry for me. *(Slight beat.)* The only thing I have, I guess, is that I live here. I'm American. And you're not. I have this country and its laws. And you don't. You have your papers, honey? You have that green card? You have a right to be standing here waiting for my bus? Using up my roads and my housing? I've seen it happen before—I've seen the company call Immigration every time there's a little agitation at the plant. Union talk. Unhappy workers. I've seen it. It's not nice. The place goes crazy when those agents appear. You see old people running pretty fast! I'd laugh—I would—I'd laugh watching those pretty legs running from the INS like a dog. *(Beat.)* I'm sorry. Forget that. Sounding like a fucking

Nazi asshole. I don't mean to make threats to you. I'm not the kind to
do that. I guess it's the only power I thought I had over you. And I
guess I don't even have that.

*(JOHN starts to leave. ALEJANDRA talks but doesn't look at JOHN.
JOHN stops, looks at ALEJANDRA.)*

ALEJANDRA. I didn't live through the worst of it: I was too
young. But I heard stories from my family. Stories always told in
whispers. *(Slight beat.)* My uncle lived in Buenos Aires. He said during the worst of it he and my aunt would hear two or three explosions
a night. The left bombing the right, the right bombing the left. And
he said he got to the point where he knew, by the sound the explosion
made, whether or not there had been a human being in the explosion.
(Slight beat.) We had a neighbor. Old man. Nice old man. A doctor.
He used to work with the military making sure the torture didn't kill
the prisoners. As a doctor he knew how to keep political prisoners
alive so the army could rape and torture more and more. The power
those men had in those rooms was absolute. They are gone—but
they are not really gone. *(She looks at him.)* Hey John: go ahead.
Send me back. Send me back.

(The two wait together. Blackout.)

THE END

IF SUSAN SMITH COULD TALK

by
ELAINE ROMERO

For Irene and George Romero

AUTHOR'S NOTE: It seems only fitting that Susan Smith's story would resonate with me after growing up in the Southwest, hearing the legend of *La Llorona* who drowned her children in the Rio Grande. She is doomed forever to roam the land, mourning her lost children. They say when the wind howls at night, it is she, crying for them, and that she can never find peace, not even in death.

IF SUSAN SMITH COULD TALK was first workshopped and performed in November 1995 in a non-equity production at the Planet Earth Multi-Cultural Theatre in Phoenix, Arizona. It was directed by **Rick Tobin** with the following cast:

Susan Smith	Victoria Hunt
Steph	Carol Anne Perini
Jerry	Shay Calinawan
Carrie	Jennifer Wright

A special thanks to **Peter James Cirino**

It was substantially revised during a subsequent production at Actors Theatre of Louisville in December 1996. **Michael Bigelow Dixon** was the Dramaturg. It was directed by **Shannon Mayers** with the following cast:

Susan Smith	Kathleen Early
Steph	Bayne Gibby
Jerry	Kimberly Gainer
Carrie	Emily Vail

Scenic Designer **Tom Burch**
Costume Designer **Kevin R. McLeod**
Lighting Designer **Laura Wickman**
Sound Designer **Elizabeth Rhodes**
Properties Designer **Mark Walston**
Stage Manager **Charles M. Turner, III**
Assistant Stage Managers **Anna Drum, Heather Fields, Daniel William Gregg**

The following disclaimer shall appear in the program notes or be posted in the theatre: *The representation of Susan Smith that the character makes is not a representation of the actual person. None of the words are actual words spoken by Susan Smith. This is a play of illustrative purpose.*

CHARACTERS

SUSAN SMITH: The young South Carolina mother who drowned her two children in the family car.
CARRIE: A judge.
STEPH: Susan's white, feminist defense attorney.
JERRY: A male African-American prosecuting attorney.

TIME
An appeal to change the sentence to death.

PLACE
A court room/execution room.

SETTING
An electric chair sits in the center. The judge sits to one side. The attorneys sit at tables on opposite sides of the electric chair.

IF SUSAN SMITH COULD TALK

(Lights up on STEPH who sits far to one side, facing the audience.)

STEPH. When I first saw Susan Smith—when I very first saw her. I saw the face of an angel. And with those gold-rimmed glasses, it was like she had some kind of vulnerability 'cause her eyes didn't work right.

(Lights down on STEPH. Lights up on JERRY across the room.)

JERRY. When I first saw Susan—Susan Smith. The first thing I didn't like was the way she said "black man." And that picture she had the cops draw up. He didn't look like any real black man to me, but a lily white woman's vision of a black man—one speck human, most part gorilla. No, not human at all.

(Lights down on JERRY. Lights up on CARRIE, the judge, who sits off-center behind a podium. A gavel rests next to her hand.)

CARRIE. I was driving home from court in my car, listening to one of those talk shows on the radio, and this woman called in to say Susan had confessed. She had just watched it on *A Current Affair.*

(Lights down on CARRIE. Lights up on JERRY.)

JERRY. I knew she was guilty the first time I saw her on the TV. She kept averting her eyes form the camera, and grasping her stomach. Didn't anybody see the meaning behind that? Like she was trying to reach back inside her body and find something in that empty womb.

(Lights down on JERRY. Lights up on STEPH.)

STEPH. Here was a woman who was realizing for maybe the first time that men weren't gonna want her. I think that's what made her snap, knowing she was young, and beautiful in her own way, but she was already soiled goods because of those two kids.

(Lights down on STEPH. Lights up on CARRIE.)

CARRIE. I thought, we've got a little Medea on our hands. You know the story of Medea, don't you? She went out to destroy somebody else, but she destroyed herself instead.

(Lights down on CARRIE. Lights up on JERRY.)

JERRY. Like she was trying to find something in that empty womb.

(Lights down on JERRY. Lights up on CARRIE.)

CARRIE. I saw her there on the TV, saying, "Bring my babies... back to me," and it's the way she slowed down before she said "back" that I knew she'd done it.

(Lights down on CARRIE. Lights up on STEPH.)

STEPH. Her eyes didn't work right.

(Lights down on STEPH. Lights up on CARRIE.)

CARRIE. And then, she added, as she stood next to that handsome ex-husband of hers, she said, "Bring them back to us, so we can be a family again."

(Lights down on CARRIE. Lights up on STEPH.)

STEPH. I saw the face of an angel.

(Lights down on STEPH. Lights up on CARRIE.)

CARRIE. That told the whole story for me. Here was a woman, abandoned by her husband, raising two kids alone. And I thought, this is perfect. She brought her husband back by saying some strange man had driven off with their children during a carjacking. But our modern Medea. I knew her story. She hated that husband of hers as much as she loved him, and this was the only way she could get revenge.

(Lights down on CARRIE. Lights up on STEPH.)

STEPH. When I first heard she'd done it. I thought, it must be because of a man. There's only one reason women do these kinds of things. They do them for love.

(Lights down on STEPH. Lights up. All freeze, except SUSAN, who paces around the courtroom and stops.)

SUSAN. *I knew what they were thinking. They'd made up their minds about me before I'd said anything. (SUSAN sits in the electric chair, moves her hands into leather wrist wraps, strapping herself to the chair. Her hair falls in her eyes. To the audience.) You all had, too. You all held judgments against me in your hearts. How can anyone living or dead get a fair roasting anymore? (CARRIE hits the gavel lightly on the podium.) I keep replaying the trial in my head everyday, trying to figure out what I really said. (Wistfully.) I have dreams. I have things I want. (CARRIE hits the gavel on the podium more loudly. SUSAN looks up. Tough.) Crack me like an egg and let me pour.*
CARRIE. *(Not hearing.)* Are you clear on what's at stake?
SUSAN. I've been sentenced to life imprisonment. I understand.
JERRY. If she were black, she wouldn't even have the luxury of appealing for life or death. You all would have fried her up long ago.
STEPH. My client would like to make her case.
CARRIE. This is an appeal to change your sentence to death,

Susan. Do you understand that?

SUSAN. Decisions have been made, I understand. I understand that decisions can be...

STEPH. Challenged.

SUSAN. *I don't like my sentence. My sentence is fucked. It doesn't let me run. Into the cracks of the asphalt. It doesn't let me seep into the holes in the earth. The sentence does not keep me fluid.*

CARRIE. So, you have nothing to say?

SUSAN. I would like to die, your Honor. I'm looking forward to it. I made a pact with my children. I freed them from the pain I would have caused them, and now I'd like to be freed from mine. I don't care what anybody ever thinks or says about me, but I saved those two little souls from everything. From the disappointment of love. I saved them. I know I've done the right thing. *(Beat.)* You may do the same for me.

(A moment. CARRIE looks at SUSAN. CARRIE nods. As the lights dim and flicker, SUSAN's body jolts slightly. Her head drops. STEPH looks at JERRY with disgust. CARRIE looks between them, unsure. JERRY starts clapping.)

JERRY. Bravo and it would have been so easy. *(SUSAN jolts her head up.)* All satisfied?

SUSAN. *I have dreams. I have things I want.*

JERRY. Your honor. She rejects your leniency.

CARRIE. Life imprisonment is lenient?

JERRY. *(Simultaneously; sarcastically.)* Or was that cruelty?

SUSAN. *(As if she's said it before.)* People don't understand. There was this man that I really loved with all my heart. But when it came time for us to get married, he said, "I can't do it. I'm not ready to take on the responsibility of being a father."

JERRY. *(Simultaneously; as if he's heard it before.)* "I'm not ready to take on the responsibility of being a father."

SUSAN. No man fathers another man's children without some resentment in the heart. And when he said that, it just shattered me because I'm beautiful, aren't I? And I don't deserve this.

(SUSAN drops her head.)

JERRY. You think you're beautiful?

(STEPH stands.)

STEPH. Let's not forget that Susan is a symbol first, a woman second. *(Catching herself.)* I mean—

SUSAN. *I stand for something else. Other than being me.*

STEPH. Her mistake is a cry—a cry from a whole society of young women who feel like Hester Prynne. Well, Susan Smith ripped that scarlet letter right off her chest.

JERRY. Your Honor, literary allusions aren't gonna save her face. She killed two innocent children. They had no choice. All those kids knew was that they were goin' on a drive with mommy, and mommy dumped them in a lake.

SUSAN. What people don't understand is that I was trying to kill myself.

JERRY. We all understand that really well. *(Beat.)* But the reality is, you failed. You drowned your kids and left precious Susan alive. Now tell me—how'd that happen?

CARRIE. Mr. Johnson.

JERRY. It's just so obvious—this woman never had a brain.

SUSAN. I made a mistake. *I have most of a brain. I can think the same thought every day for the rest of my life. (A mantra.) I killed them. I killed them.*

JERRY. You didn't breathe a word until you knew you'd been caught, and the press announced on national television there were holes in your story.

SUSAN. *The press announced on national television there were holes in my head.*

CARRIE. *(Simultaneously.)* Mr. Johnson, that's enough.

STEPH. It's really easy for Mr. Johnson to be self-righteous. But we all know that Mr. Johnson will never know what it's like to be a young and scared single mom.

SUSAN. *Mr. Johnson will never know what it's like to be your step-dad's favorite...*

JERRY. *(Simultaneously.)* I know what it's like to be a black man. She accused all of us, you know.

SUSAN. *His favorite __daughter__. (Retreating.)* If I'd committed suicide, I would have left them motherless and that wouldn't have been right.

JERRY. So, it's better to kill them?

SUSAN. *(Venom.) His favorite fuck.*

STEPH. *(Loudly.)* Your honor, the death penalty.

(CARRIE pounds the gavel.)

CARRIE. Order in the court.

SUSAN. *My step-father is not on trial here. He is not on trial.* *(Beat; catatonic.)* Children can't live without their mothers. It's a known fact. *I know I wouldn't be who I am today if it weren't for my parents.*

CARRIE. Susan.

SUSAN. I loved my babies more than anything. I never wanted anything bad to happen to them, and noting ever will. 'Cause I've spared them. And you don't know how that makes me feel as a murderer—I mean, a mother.

JERRY. Your honor, Susan suffers from delusions. No matter what anybody tells her, she sees this whole thing through her own twisted eyes—and in those eyes, she's always the heroine.

STEPH. She feels she has saved her children because something— something about this world has been too painful for her.

SUSAN. *My step-father chomped me down bit by bit. He was a criminal that way. He liked to eat people.*

STEPH. Say something. Describe your pain.

SUSAN. *My step-father swallowed my tongue. If he hadn't, you'd hear me.*

CARRIE. Susan, don't you want to say anything in your defense? Something that will help us understand?

SUSAN. *(Not a response.)* I've been talkin' to my babies. They've forgiven me. I've talked to God and he's forgiven me, too. *Every day.* People from the world yell at me through their TVs. They'll never feel anything for me but hatred.

JERRY. Your Honor, Susan Smith does not have a repentant heart. I doubt Susan Smith has a heart at all.

STEPH. I ask that my client be put to death at her request. To stop the pain.

CARRIE. You suggest the death penalty as a painkiller?

JERRY. Life imprisonment. Let her count the days.

SUSAN. *Have you ever cried and no one listened?*

STEPH. Listen to her words.

SUSAN. *No one hears me.* A couple days before I sank to that lowest point, my oldest was playing, hanging from my neck. His hands felt like ropes around me.

JERRY. Your Honor, this is preposterous.

SUSAN. My oldest lived a happy two years and my youngest, a blessed fourteen months. Nobody's gonna take that time from us. Sure, I could have killed them bit by bit. But I did it fast and quick and without a lot of pain.

JERRY. Your babies suffered. You watched your eldest try to get out of the car seat.

SUSAN. I was crying too much to watch, sir.

JERRY. You were so tearful you went on national television going on about some black man when all the time it was you.

SUSAN. I know.

JERRY. You lied to every sympathetic heart in this country.

SUSAN. I wanted to live.

JERRY. I thought you wanted to kill yourself.

SUSAN. *(Stronger.)* I wanted to live.

JERRY. So, you lied to save your ass.

SUSAN. I lied to start over. With him. I'm giving you my second chance.

STEPH. My client wants to be free. She wants to die.

JERRY. This young woman is a murderess. *(Short beat.)* This whole death penalty thing is just a complicated suicide. She wants to get us to kill her because she never had the courage to do it herself.

SUSAN. You're right. I never had the courage.

(A pound of the gavel.)

CARRIE. Sentence stands. Life. No parole.

SUSAN. No! *(Beat.) Sacrifices made for love are never understood by the people inside the TV who pound the gavel loud and hard, especially human sacrifices made for helium balloons who want to live in castles on the hill. (Beat.) I was going to be his princess—*

I was going to be his queen. Put a pin in me, so I'll pop.

(CARRIE crosses to SUSAN and frees SUSAN's hands from the wrist wraps. STEPH looks at JERRY with disgust. CARRIE looks between them, unsure. Blackout.)

THE END

A Paranoid Sexual
Fantasy in Ten Minutes

by

JOHN SHEEHY

GAVE HER THE EYE
by **John Sheehy**

Directed by **Jeanine DeFalco**
Dramaturg **Charles Forbes**

Donna ....Bayne Gibby
Dex ....Eric Keith
Clarissa ....Anne Marie Nest

Scenic Designer **Tom Burch**
Costume Designer **Rebecca Trout**
Lighting Designer **Laura Wickman**
Sound Designer **Elizabeth Rhodes**
Properties Manager **Mark Walston**
Stage Manager **Charles M. Turner, III**
Assistant Stage Managers **Anna Drum, Heather Fields,**
Daniel William Gregg

GAVE HER THE EYE

(A Bar. DONNA, still dressed from work, sits alone at one table. Towards the back CLARISSA, dressed a little cheaply, sits alone at another table. DEX, also dressed from work, enters with a couple of drinks.)

DEX. Here we go.

DONNA. Oh, thank God.

DEX. There. *(She sips.)* Is it all right?

DONNA. Oh, yeah, fine.

DEX. Thanks for coming out with me.

DONNA. Oh, sure.

DEX. You didn't totally want to, hunh?

DONNA. No, hey, I...

DEX. No, that's okay, I mean I appreciate that. It's a good sign.

DONNA. Really? A good sign?

DEX. Yeah. *(Pause.)* Can I ask you a question?

DONNA. Of course.

DEX. I mean, it's kind of personal.

DONNA. Oh... uh... sure.

DEX. It is also... kind of... vitally important.

DONNA. Well, Jesus...

DEX. You swear you'll give me a straight answer?

DONNA. If I can, I guess.

DEX. Listen. *(He checks that no one is listening in.)* You are a human being aren't you?

DONNA. Yeah...

DEX. No, I mean—You are human?

DONNA. Yes.

DEX. I mean 100%.

DONNA. Yes, what do you...?

DEX. I'm sorry but...

DONNA. Look, maybe this wasn't a good idea...

DEX. No, no, I'm sorry. I know this is sounding weird.

DONNA. No, no... it's me. I'm just not used to... being quizzed on, like, my species, you know?

DEX. If you'll let me explain...

DONNA. I don't think...

DEX. Please, let me show you something.

DONNA. I... um... definitely don't want you showing me anything, all right? I think I better go.

DEX. Five minutes. Please. Really, it's important. I don't know how much time I actually have.

DONNA. Hey, I thought you were some kind of normal guy, you know?

DEX. So did I.

DONNA. Well, there you go.

(She starts to exit, he stops her.)

DEX. No... it's just... I thought I was normal, too, a couple days ago. Here just sit down. Give me a couple of minutes and let me show you something. Please, please. I'm not going to hurt you or anything. Please? *(She begrudgingly sits back down.)* Now, I'm going to show you something but you have to stay calm.

DONNA. Listen, I try not to get involved in situations where people feel it's necessary to tell me to stay calm.

DEX. Five minutes, please.

DONNA. All right.

DEX. *(He takes out a pair of sunglasses.)* Now, here, anybody looking?

(They both check around. When the coast is clear, he takes out one of his eyeballs and immediately puts on the sunglasses.)

DONNA. What? What are you doing?

DEX. Relax. Here, look at this.

(He hands her the eye.)

DONNA. Mother of God!

DEX. Shhhhhhh! Calm down. Don't drop it.

DONNA. I got to go.

DEX. Donna, please. You may be the only person I can trust.

DONNA. What is this?

DEX. My eye.

DONNA. I can see that!

DEX. Keep it down.

DONNA. Easy for you to say.

DEX. Just... look at it. It's not human. Look at it. Careful, don't let anyone see you. Look at the back of it. See those electronic connection things at the back?

DONNA. Jesus!

DEX. One morning, I just popped it out. I was standing at the sink. I felt like hell. There was this big office party. I don't remember half of it. Hung over, or so I thought. I had all this gunk in my eye and I was washing my face, trying to clean up. I was rubbing my eye right there, you know, in the corner of my eye and I heard this loud click in my head and my eye just came right out in my hand.

DONNA. I'm going to be sick.

DEX. Yeah, you don't want to see the socket. It's like all covered with these fiber optic connection points. They did something to me.

DONNA. They?

DEX. Yeah.

DONNA. They who?

DEX. How do I know?

DONNA. What is all this?

DEX. I know this sounds crazy.

DONNA. Sounds crazy? No, more like flat out crazy.

DEX. They are turning me into a machine, like all the rest.

DONNA. Oh, shut up. Like all the rest...

DEX. No, listen... When I put my eye out, that first time, I was like totally freaking. I mean I was running out the door, half-dressed, when I suddenly remembered this like dream from the night before.

I mean, I thought it had to be like some kind of dream, right, but then I started to remember the actual, you know, sensations of coming to in a hospital bed in the middle of some kind of operation on my head.

DONNA. Gross...

DEX. Yeah, and everyone is like shitting that I'm coming to, people are running and yelling at each other, then I guess someone gave me a shot and I was out again. But I remember Kathleen, you know, the Branch Manager, pitching a fit to kill. I mean she was bitching out this doctor about how "80% of the district had been successfully replaced, and if you jeopardize that by screwing up this one simple accountant replacement..."

DONNA. This is way to whacked for me.

DEX. I know, I know. I thought I was going crazy.

DONNA. Hold the thought!

DEX. No! I mean, look me in the eye and tell me this is normal.

DONNA. Which one?

DEX. I need you. You are the only person I can turn to...

DONNA. Me? You are a one-eyed nut!

DEX. Look, people are being replaced. Think about it. Think of the people you know.

DONNA. I hardly know anyone. I just moved here.

DEX. I know, that's why you are probably the only person here I can trust. Think of the people at work. You are like the only person there that makes any mistakes...

DONNA. Hey!

DEX. No, not big ones. Little ones. Little slip-ups, like misplacing messages, forgetting something on your desk and having to go back for it. Little things. But no one else even seems to blink in that place. Look, all I'm saying, I am being changed, and while I am not completely human anymore... I... uh... I do know that there are... parts of me that still work the way they always did, if you know what I mean?

DONNA. I'm gone.

DEX. Listen, I may be the only man that knows that this is going on. Clearly, I was never intended to know as much as I do, but nothing can be done about that now... I just... Look, I'm scared, okay? I am really scared and I figure, you, you, you're too new to have been changed and I... I... just need a little human contact.

DONNA. Not from this human.

DEX. Don't dismiss this. Please, just promise me, think about it. And for your safety and mine, don't mention this to anyone. *(He takes back his eye.)* I better put this back in before it gets too dry. Please think about it.

(He exits.)

DONNA. Mother of God!

(She downs her drink. She starts to leave but sits back down, starts again but only gets about as far as CLARISSA.)

CLARISSA. *(High pitched squeaky voice.)* Ah, go ahead.

DONNA. Excuse me?

CLARISSA. Stick around. Wait for him.

DONNA. I don't think I should...

CLARISSA. Oh, come on! It's not the end of the world. You think he's cute? He likes you. Wait for him.

DONNA. If it's not the end of the world then I'm definitely not waiting for him.

CLARISSA. Sit down, here. Look, may I speak? I saw him give you the eye.

DONNA. I... I... I... I...

CLARISSA. Calm down. Don't get yourself in a spin! It's a trick. It's like a toy or something. His eye? My foot! Can you believe the extent to which some men will go these days to avoid wearing a condom...

DONNA. What? Wearing a... what...?

CLARISSA. Didn't he give you the whole, we-must-procreate-and-save-the-world number?

DONNA. Not exactly...

CLARISSA. He does want to sleep with you, doesn't he?

DONNA. Yeah, but it was more of a you-and-me-against-the-alien-robots number.

CLARISSA. Hunh! Changing it up a bit? Not bad. It's still crap, but it's new crap. He's not resting on his laurels... Anyway, there is no conspiracy, no invasion or whatever he told you.

DONNA. I... don't believe this... I semi-believed him.

CLARISSA. Yeah, well, he's cute and seems nice. It's so crazy... who would believe he was making it up. But you know what... leave if you want... but if you stay, I doubt you'll be sorry. I mean he is really good, like top ten good, and I should know, if you now what I mean? So, stick around, have fun, you can be careful, take precautions...

DONNA. This is probably the sickest thing that has ever happened to me!

CLARISSA. You're young, give it time...

DONNA. I am definitely out of here!

(DONNA storms out. CLARISSA looks around, takes a cellular phone from her purse and dials, waits.)

CLARISSA. *(Normal voice.)* Yeah, it's me. He just tried it again. We've got to pick him up tonight. I got a couple of shots of the girl... Yeah... no we can just eliminate her... Yes, tonight, definitely.

(She hangs up. Blackout.)

THE END

AT SEA

by

MAYO SIMON

AT SEA
by **Mayo Simon**

Directed by **Risa Brainin**

Hal ....Brian Carter
Edie ....April Golden

Dramaturg **Spencer Parsons**
Stage Manager **Jen Wills**
Technical Director **Frazier Marsh**
Lighting Designer **Steve O'Shea**
Sound Designer **Shane Rettig**
Costume Designer **Kevin McLeod**

CHARACTERS

HAL
EDIE

AT SEA

(HAL in a bathing suit sitting on a kitchen chair, moving his arm as though swimming with a one-armed stroke. EDIE in a bathing suit sitting next to HAL on a kitchen chair, holding his thigh with a dainty hand. Her other hand holds up the novel she is reading. On the other side of HAL, on a kitchen chair, is a bucket of water. For several moments HAL swims silently, breathing heavily. EDIE reads. Finally HAL speaks.)

HAL. How you doing?
EDIE. Okay.

(HAL keeps on swimming, breathing heavily.)

HAL. You okay?
EDIE. Yes, fine.
HAL. Good. That's real good. *(HAL keeps on swimming.)* No problems?
EDIE. No, no.
HAL. Okay. *(HAL keeps on swimming.)* Comfortable?
EDIE. What?
HAL. Are you comfortable?
EDIE. Hal, you can see I'm reading.
HAL. Oh, sorry.

(HAL continues swimming. EDIE looks up.)

EDIE. You're doing really well.

HAL. Thank you. *(HAL's head falls into the bucket of water. After a few moments, his head jerks out again.)* What happened?

EDIE. You had a little lapse.

HAL. Oh. You all right?

EDIE. I'm fine.

HAL. That's good.

(HAL starts swimming again.)

EDIE. You're doing really hard stuff.

HAL. Well, I'm doing all the swimming. *(EDIE smiles, goes back to her novel. HAL swims, breathing heavily, then he continues.)* Say, listen, Edie. You remember back before we started we had that talk. Remember, I said it would be impossible for me to do all the swimming forever? I had done it in the past, and I just couldn't do it anymore? You remember me saying that. And you said not to worry, no problem, things were going to be different from now on. And I said maybe we should discuss it a little more before we start, and you said no it's all settled. Well now I find it's not settled at all. In fact, it's the same story, Edie. I do all the swimming.

EDIE. So?

HAL. Well, we had an agreement, don't you remember?

EDIE. Why do you use that tone of voice?

HAL. What tone of voice?

EDIE. That sarcastic tone.

HAL. Edie, I'm not being sarcastic. I'm just a little stressed.

EDIE. And you're talking really loud. That scares me. My ex-husband yelled at me all the time, I was terrified of him.

HAL. I'm sorry, Edie. I'll watch myself in the future.

EDIE. Thank you.

(EDIE returns to her reading. HAL swims.)

HAL. We did have an agreement. *(Silence.)* Do you remember our agreement? *(Silence.)* I'm asking you a question, Edie.

EDIE. Why do you keep bringing this up?

HAL. Because I'm getting exhausted here.

EDIE. Oh, stop exaggerating.

(HAL's head falls in the bucket of water. After a few moments his head jerks out again.)

HAL. What happened?
EDIE. You had a little lapse.
HAL. Oh. *(Treading water.)* You all right?
EDIE. I'm fine.
HAL. Then why don't you swim a little?
EDIE. Hal, what's your problem?
HAL. Edie, can't you see I need help?
EDIE. I'm not a mind reader, Hal.
HAL. Well, I'm telling you.
EDIE. All right then.
HAL. Okay.
EDIE. I fully intend to help.

(HAL continues swimming. EDIE continues reading her novel.)

HAL. But you don't.
EDIE. Hal, I understand. I do. I really do. I should have known how important this was to you. I just goofed up. I'm really sorry. All right?
HAL. Well, yeah. But you're not swimming.
EDIE. Why are you pressuring me?
HAL. I'm not pressuring you, I'm just reminding you that if you don't swim a little I'm probably going to drown.
EDIE. I have to be my own person, Hal.
HAL. Edie, believe me, you are your own person.
EDIE. You may not realize, but it's very difficult for me here. This is a very strange environment for me. Sometimes I feel like I'm losing my identity.
HAL. Well, it's a strange environment for me too.
EDIE. I don't think you realize how important this is. I spent years trying to find myself. Now I feel if I did what you told me to every minute, I would just disappear.
HAL. I don't want you to disappear.
EDIE. Then you have to be very careful when you talk to me.

(HAL's head falls in the bucket of water. After a moment, it jerks up again.)

HAL. What happened?

EDIE. Nothing.

HAL. You all right, sweetheart?

EDIE. I'm fine.

HAL. Well, sweetheart, darling, how long do you think it will be before you can swim a little?

EDIE. I need time.

HAL. Oh, Okay. Time for what?

EDIE. If you must know, you make me nervous.

HAL. I make you nervous?

EDIE. Yes.

HAL. How do I make you nervous?

EDIE. I don't think you like the way I swim. I don't know if I should do a dog paddle or swim on my back or what?

HAL. Edie, have I ever discussed the way you swim?

EDIE. No.

HAL. Then why not swim any way you want.

EDIE. You are a very critical person, Hal. You are sarcastic and you are critical and you are demanding and you want everything your way. You may not know it, but that's the way you are.

HAL. I don't agree.

EDIE. Well, you should think about it.

HAL. All right, I'll think about it. And while I'm thinking about it maybe you could swim a little. *(Silence. HAL treads water.)* Edie, didn't we have an agreement?

EDIE. This is a control issue.

(HAL's head falls in the bucket of water. He comes up sputtering.)

HAL. What are you talking about?

EDIE. Why are you trying to control me?

HAL. I am not trying to control you. We made an agreement. We discussed it and we agreed. What's the point of making an agreement if you don't live up to it?

EDIE. I don't want a solution, Hal. I want you to listen to me. I don't think you value me very highly. I don't think you hear what I say.

HAL. Edie, what you say is bullshit. You didn't swim before and you're not swimming now and you always have one more reason not to do anything.

EDIE. You have a problem, Hal.

HAL. No, you have a problem, Edie.

EDIE. No, you have a problem, Hal.

HAL. You know you remind me of my ex. Pretty soon we can have the which-one-of-us-is-crazy argument. *(EDIE starts to cry.)* What's wrong now?

EDIE. I'm scared if I don't do what you want, you'll abandon me.

HAL. I'm not going to abandon you. But I am totally frustrated. If I don't say anything, you do nothing and you say you're not a mind reader. But if I say something to you, it's a control issue and you still won't do anything. Whatever I say or don't say is wrong.

EDIE. *(Giggling.)* You have a point there.

HAL. Yes, I think I do.

EDIE. All right, tell me what's bothering you.

HAL. Edie, we had an agreement which you ignore. And we have a practical situation that I can't make any headway with you about.

EDIE. Well, this is just not a good time for me.

HAL. *(Treading water, choking.)* Well, it's not a good time for me either. In fact, this is sort of an emergency for me.

EDIE. Can we take it up when I'm finished reading?

HAL. Can you read a little later?

EDIE. If you ever listened to me, Hal, you'd know that reading is very important to me. It reminds me of who I am. I can't just give it up.

HAL. Edie, in one minute you're going to make me scream.

EDIE. Hal, why don't you think of all the good things I do for you?

(HAL's head falls into the bucket of water. For several moments, nothing happens. Then he comes up choking.)

HAL. Goddamnit, Edie, I can't take this anymore! It's over my head! Do you hear me?

EDIE. Why are you so angry?

HAL. Because I'm drowning and you won't swim!

EDIE. Hal, I have an idea.

HAL. Tell me, what?

EDIE. Why don't we swim by ourselves for a while.

HAL. Swim by ourselves?

EDIE. Yes.

HAL. You swim by yourself and I swim by myself? And I don't have to pull you along?

EDIE. That's my idea.

HAL. Well, okay.

EDIE. Good.

HAL. Just one thing.

EDIE. Yes?

HAL. We could end up drifting apart.

EDIE. *(To the heavens above.)* Can I never do anything right?

HAL. No, no. Edie. Wait. Listen. *(She turns back.)* If that's the best we can do, all right, that's what we'll do. We'll swim apart. Okay. When do we start?

EDIE. Any time.

HAL. Like now?

EDIE. Absolutely.

HAL. Okay. *(HAL continues swimming. EDIE stops reading, stares straight ahead. Her hand, still on his thigh, begins to shake. HAL goes on, gasping for air.)* Edie?

EDIE. Yes, Hal?

HAL. Edie... I've thought about this a lot... and I think... you just don't want to swim.

EDIE. You have to win every argument, don't you?

HAL. That has nothing to do with it.

EDIE. Yes, you just have to win, no matter what. That's how men are. *(HAL looks at her, then starts to slip off the chair. EDIE grabs him. They embrace.)* Are you all right, sweetheart?

HAL. I'm really tired.

EDIE. You should ease up on yourself.

HAL. I'll try.

(HAL's head falls into the bucket of water.)

EDIE. Hal? *(He does not move.)* I love you very much.

(HAL's head jerks up for a moment.)

HAL. Love you too. *(His head falls back in the bucket of water. Moments pass. EDIE puts down the book. She grabs HAL's shoulder and starts swimming vigorously with a one-armed back stroke. HAL's head comes out of the bucket, talking.)* No, no, no, that's all wrong, that's not right, you're not breathing through your mouth, you have to kick, you have to dig in, is the back stroke really your best stroke? I doubt it, I don't think so, of course who am I to tell you anything?

(EDIE lets go of his shoulder. His head falls back in the bucket. She sighs.)

EDIE. I think I'll get something else to read.

(She moves her arm as though swimming. HAL's head remains in the bucket. EDIE hums a defiant tune. The lights fade. The play is over.)

THE END

THE LEAGUE OF
SEMI-SUPERHEROES

by

VAL SMITH
and
MICHAEL BIGELOW DIXON

THE LEAGUE OF SEMI-SUPERHEROES
by **Val Smith** and **Michael Bigelow Dixon**
Directed by **Michael Bigelow Dixon**
Dramaturg **Charles Forbes**

Carol ....Emily Vail
El Grande De Sayer De Nay ....Scott Parrish
Master of the Obvious ....Briton Green
Pushy Bob ....Jared Randolph
Wabbit Woman ....Miriam Brown
The Human Puddle ....David L. Ray

Scenic Designer **Tom Burch**
Costume Designer **Rebecca Trout**
Lighting Designer **Laura Wickman**
Sound Designer **Josh T. Wirtz**
Properties Designer **Mark Walston**
Stage Manager **Charles M. Turner, III**
Assistant Stage Managers **Anna Drum, Heather Fields,
Daniel William Gregg**

THE LEAGUE—DREAMERS ALL, BUT REAL, VERY REAL
EL GRANDE DE SAYER DE NAY
MASTER OF THE OBVIOUS
PUSHY BOB
WABBIT WOMAN
THE HUMAN PUDDLE
and
CAROL, the League Receptionist
TIME
Oh, who cares
PLACE
The LEAGUE OF SEMI-SUPERHEROES' sparsely furnished office.
A spartan desk with chair. The desk is noticeably devoid of papers or
implements of any kind. The only object is a gold glittery phone with
wings—and an answering machine. Mayber there's something else
to sit on in the office, but it's not a normal piece of furniture. Some
good rousing "SuperHero" pre-show theme music is in order.

THE LEAGUE OF SEMI-SUPERHEROES

(AT RISE, the gold telephone is highlighted. It rings. The answering machine picks up. CAROL enters, but makes no effort to pick up the phone. Instead she busies herself with putting away her coat, her purse, and shopping bags, putting on lipstick, and picking up and looking through the mail, all under the following.)

CAROL'S VOICE. Hello. You have reached the number of The League of Semi-Superheroes. If this is an emergency, please stay on the line and an operator will pick up shortly. *(Pause.)* If this is a message for only The Human Puddle, please press "1" now. *(Pause. The HUMAN PUDDLE flies in the door, listening intently. When the message goes on to the next Semi-Super Hero, THE HUMAN PUDDLE bursts into tears, just as WABBIT WOMAN hops into the room with her snorkel. Smocking, she smirks in anticipation.)* If this is a message for Wabbit Woman, please press "2" now.

WABBIT WOMAN. *(Pause.)* Oh wats!

VOICE. If this is a message for Master of the Obvious, please press "3" now.

(MASTER OF THE OBVIOUS has entered the room, all smiles.)

MASTER OF THE OBVIOUS. Hey!! We got a call?

(Pause. EL GRANDE DE SAYER DE NAY enters frowning as usual.)

VOICE. If this is a message for El Grande De Sayer De Nay, *(pause)*...

EL GRANDE. *(A look of hope then cynicism and simultaneously with tape.)* ... don't bother to press anything.

VOICE. ... don't bother to press anything. If this is a message for Pushy Bob, press "4"—

PUSHY BOB. Yow! Watch out!

(PUSHY BOB blasts through the doorway, scattering everybody.)

VOICE. —and get out of the way. If this is a message for the entire League, please leave it at the tone—

(THE LEAGUE leans in eagerly to listen. The sound of the tone. There is the sound of snorts and giggles, and then a hang-up.)

EL GRANDE DE SAYER. Told ya.

THE HUMAN PUDDLE. It could have been something. It might have been something.

EL GRANDE. They only call 'cause they think we're a joke.

(HUMAN PUDDLE bursts into tears.)

MASTER OF THE OBVIOUS. You've upset The Puddle.

EL GRANDE. So what else is new?

WABBIT WOMAN. *(Through snorkel she sings "Rain Drops are Falling on My Head.")*

PUSHY BOB. So! Carol, whaddaya doin'? What are you working on there?

CAROL. *(Working on her crossword puzzle.)* Oh, I don't know, Pushy Bob. What does it look like to you?

MASTER OF THE OBVIOUS. Say, isn't that a crossword puzzle you've got there?

CAROL. I'm surrounded. I give up.

PUSHY BOB. *(Looking over CAROL's shoulder.)* Oh, way-way-way-way-wait! Forty-four down, a five letter word for "screw-up"! Hold on, hold on. No, hold on now, hold on! Ahhhhh—

CAROL. *(Grabbing crossword puzzle back from PUSHY BOB.)* Look! Instead of working MY crossword puzzle, why don't we deal with your bills? For instance. Here. The bank statement. Oh, my.

Surprise, surprise. You're overdrawn on all your accounts.

MASTER OF THE OBVIOUS. Ooh bummer.

CAROL. Exactly. Ooh bummer. And what is this? Why, it's an eviction notice from the landlord. Oh dear. What should you do? Any semi-super money to take care of this? Any semi-super ideas? Any ideas at all? *(An embarrassed silence among the Semi-Super Heroes.)* No? Well then, there's a little matter of my salary. You are familiar with the word "salary?" Money in exchange for work provided?

MASTER OF THE OBVIOUS. Ah c'mon Carol. We know what salary means.

PUSHY BOB. Hey, we'll write you a check!

CAROL. I'll start clearing out my desk.

MASTER OF THE OBVIOUS. Our bank account is overdrawn.

(CAROL begins emptying out her desk, collecting her personal belongings in a box. PUSHY BOB hovers around her, checking out her stuff.)

WABBIT WOMAN. Hizth izth ridiculuzzz! *(Without snorkel.)* They can't take away our *office*, for cwying out wowed. How will we do ouh bidness?

EL GRANDE DE SAYER. Look around, Wabbit Woman. Don't you see? *(They ALL look around.)* Oh, c'mon! All of you? Any of you? Don't you see?

(Puzzled, they ALL look round again.)

WABBIT WOMAN. Well. We're wookin'—

EL GRANDE DE SAYER. I'm speaking metaphorically!

MASTER OF THE OBVIOUS. No fair! You can't expect *me* to figure that out.

WABBIT WOMAN. He's Master of the Obvious.

EL GRANDE DE SAYER. Don't you see, it isn't working! We *have* no business! In a year, nobody has called for our services. It can't work! It will never work! Never, never, never!

(The HUMAN PUDDLE sobs loudly.)

MASTER OF THE OBVIOUS. Geez. There goes The Puddle.

EL GRANDE. Oh what else is new!

PUSHY BOB. Look out everybody! The glass is half empty again.

EL GRANDE DE SAYER. This time it's completely empty. We're being evicted. Carol is thinking of leaving.

CAROL. Correction. Carol *is* leaving. *(To PUSHY BOB.)* Will you *please* get out of the way!

PUSHY BOB. Okay! Have a big gigantic ding-dong cow!

EL GRANDE DE SAYER. I mean, who are we kidding? "Semi-Super Heroes!" Our talents make no sense!

CAROL. Finally. Thank you, God.

THE HUMAN PUDDLE. Ordinary people with "unusual" skills helping other people in need.

MASTER OF THE OBVIOUS. That was the whole idea.

EL GRANDE DE SAYER. Sounds good, Human Puddle. Only one problem. Who *needs* stupid skills?

WABBIT WOMAN. Ma skiffs ant stoofid! *(Removes snorkel from mouth.)* Can you smock, snorkel AND smirk? I can!

EL GRANDE DE SAYER. Who cares?

MASTER OF THE OBVIOUS. It may not be obvious to everyone but even if it is—doesn't it follow, El Grande de Sayer de Nay, that you also have a stupid skill?

ALL. Hmmmmmmmmmmmmmm?!

El GRANDE DE SAYER. NO!

ALL. Oh.

CAROL. Guys, there's one more piece of...

PUSHY BOB. Look! Right now, somebody out there might *need* a pushy guy! And if I can help by bulldozing my way in somewhere, hey—I'm there!

HUMAN PUDDLE. Or just someone who likes to—who can't help—crying—

(THE HUMAN PUDDLE sobs uncontrollably.)

CAROL. Guys, you're not listening.

WABBIT WOMAN. We're wisionaries!

EL GRANDE DE SAYER. We're the League of Personality Disorders!

MASTER OF THE OBVIOUS. Some people choose not to see it that way. While others obviously do.

PUSHY BOB. I've always thought we could use more aggressive advertising. Loud and In Your Face.

WABBIT WOMAN. Yah! *Willwe* Wowed!

PUSHY BOB. Yeah! Willwe willwe Wowed!

CAROL. Guys. If I could have your attention a...

PUSHY BOB. Ah! "Gaffe"! Five letters meaning "screw-up"—could work.

CAROL. Thank you, Pushy Bob! I wanted to spare everyone's feelings, but there is one more piece of information I need to share with you. The Grant? *(The group looks puzzled.)* Remember The Grant? *(The group looks puzzled.)* The last glint of rescue in an otherwise dark sea of despair?

(HUMAN PUDDLE weeps, a high-pitched sob.)

PUSHY BOB. *(A flash.)* Oh! Yeah! The Grant! *(He knocks CAROL's box off the desk accidentally.)* Helping people with our unusual skills!

CAROL. Well. You didn't get The Grant.

WABBIT WOMAN. Ooooooooooooooooo.

THE HUMAN PUDDLE. Oh God! How much rejection do they think we can take?!

MASTER OF THE OBVIOUS. Maybe the word "semi-" gave them pause.

EL GRANDE DE SAYER. That's it! I, El Grande De Sayer de Nay, propose we disband!

WABBIT WOMAN. Ooooooooooooooooooooooooooooooo.

EL GRANDE DE SAYER. You heard me! Quit! We follow Carol on out of here.

CAROL. I walk alone!

MASTER OF THE OBVIOUS. You mean—give up the office.

WABBIT WOMAN. Look. We have to have faith. Faith that somehow our talents, howevah stwange, howevah cweative, howevah—meager—amount to something. I'm not giving up smocking for nobody. I'll continue to smock—and smirk—and, yes!, snorkel wheorbel I foltb libit.

MASTER OF THE OBVIOUS. Smock on, Wabbit Woman!

HUMAN PUDDLE. We just wanted to help people.

PUSHY BOB. Well, what the hell do people want! I mean, excuse me for illuminating the human condition but we do so have something to offer! Can't they see that?!

MASTER OF THE OBVIOUS. Push on, Pushy Bob!

EL GRANDE DE SAYER. No! This is the end. We have to accept that. We have to be big enough to say "yes" to "no!"

(A moment while they all ponder this statement.)

MASTER OF THE OBVIOUS. We didn't get our grant.

PUSHY BOB. And who's to blame? *(Pause.)* Carol. We'll miss you. You're fired.

CAROL. Thank you, Pushy Bob. Look guys. I'm sorry. But there is such a thing as appreciating the reality of a situation.

(Pause.)

EL GRANDE DE SAYER. Exactly, Carol! Reality! When we walk out that door, we must know who we are, and always will be—unwanted, useless, distracting, irritating, unloved and unlovable strangeohs. When we walk out that door, we're gonna know we face a world that has no use for us and our hopeless, pathetic little lives!

(EL GRANDE has rested his case. Stunned silence. After a moment, THE HUMAN PUDDLE sobs loudly. A pause.)

CAROL. Well. Let me put it this way. I've enjoyed my time here, but I never really understood how smocking and snorkeling and crying and being pushy and telling people what they already know—or being negative on a continual basis—I mean, how are those qualities supposed to help other people? Huh?

(Pause.)

WABBIT WOMAN. OK. It's a wittle weird. But is that any weason to weject us?!

CAROL. Yes. Yes, it is. (*Pause during which the lights flicker and then go out.*) Well, there it is. Reality. Third and final notice from the electric company. Tell ya what. I'll take the answering machine in lieu of a check. (*CAROL disconnects the answering machine and tucks it under her arm.*) Good luck to all of you. And I really mean that.

(*CAROL exits.*)

THE LEAGUE. (*Sadly.*) 'Bye, Carol. Bye...
MASTER OF THE OBVIOUS. She's gone.
EL GRANDE DE SAYER. We don't need her.
PUSHY BOB. She left her crossword puzzle.
WABBIT WOMAN. (*Sings another chorus of "Raindrops" sadly through snorkel.*)

(*Long pause. The phone rings. They all look at it. It rings again.*)

MASTER OF THE OBVIOUS. Phone's ringing.

(*Phone rings.*)

HUMAN PUDDLE. Aren't you going to answer it?
EL GRANDE DE SAYER. No.
PUSHY BOB. Just another noxious nincompoop lookin' for a cheap laugh. Prob'ly.

(*Phone rings.*)

HUMAN PUDDLE. But what if...
EL GRANDE DE SAYER. What!!

(*Evocative heroic music plays quietly under the following, slowing building as it progresses.*)

HUMAN PUDDLE. Well, what if it's a guy in Sault Ste. Marie who's in big trouble 'cause he can't accept what's happening in his life.
MASTER OF THE OBVIOUS. He needs help hearing some hard—but obvious—truths.

(Phone rings.)

HUMAN PUDDLE. Or, like, what if it's some shy kid in Cheyenne, who never gets picked when they're choosing up teams and never gets called on in class, who's always last in line and who always walks home alone.

PUSHY BOB. Maybe all she needs is an assertive role-model, a little jolt of brass, somebody to tell her not to be afraid to just barge in and make it happen.

(Phone rings.)

HUMAN PUDDLE. What if it's a guy in St. Louis who can't say "no" to a boss who keeps making him stay late to work and that's ruining his home life.

EL GRANDE. He needs help, he needs someone who can help him see the importance of saying "No!" Emphatically. And often.

(Phone rings.)

HUMAN PUDDLE. Or maybe it's—uhhhh—maybe it's—uhhhhh—

(HUMAN PUDDLE turns to the rest of the League in his desperation—)

PUSHY, GRANDE, MASTER & PUDDLE. Or maybe it's—uhhhhhh—

WABBIT WOMAN. A synchwonized swim team!—who want a cewtain fashion nostalgia to their swimsuits!—And who despwately need to—learn to—you know—smirk for the judges!

(Phone rings.)

HUMAN PUDDLE. Or maybe, just maybe, it's a bunch of people right here in this city. A group of dreamers who've lost their way. And maybe what they need most of all, maybe all they need in fact, is just a darn good—*(dissolving in tears.)*

(The phone keeps ringing. THE LEAGUE OF SEMI-SUPERHE-ROES, some with a look of hope, some anxious and teary, watch the phone which continues to ring as HUMAN PUDDLE looks heavenward and WABBIT WOMAN hops toward the phone ever so slowly as lights go to Black and music swells to terrific climax.)

THE END

THE UNINTENDED VIDEO

by

DALE GRIFFITHS STAMOS

THE UNINTENDED VIDEO
by Dale Griffiths Stamos

Directed by **Allyn Chandler**
Dramaturg **Charles Forbes**

Samuel ....Rick Galiher
Clarissa ....Christine Carroll

Scenic Designer **Tom Burch**
Costume Designer **Kevin R. McLeod**
Lighting Designer **Laura Wickman**
Sound Designer **Josh T. Wirtz**
Properties Designer **Mark Walston**
Stage Manager **Charles M. Turner, III**
Assistant Stage Managers **Anna Drum, Heather Fields,
Daniel William Gregg**

CAST OF CHARACTERS

SAMUEL. In his forties, a burn victim.
CLARISSA. In her late thirties, a tourist from Los Angeles.

SCENE
A park bench in a Seattle, Washington park.

TIME
The present.

THE UNINTENDED VIDEO

(SETTING: A park bench in a large Seattle park.)
(AT RISE: The sound of many birds swooping and cooing. As lights come up, we see a man, SAMUEL, seated on the bench with a bag of crumbs in his hand that he is throwing out to birds. We notice two things about SAMUEL. First, even though it is a chilly day, he is unusually covered up. He has a hat pulled low over his fore-head, and a muffler around his neck and part of his chin. Second, most of the skin that is exposed is severely scarred. He is obvi-ously a burn victim. He darts a few glances around him to make sure he's alone, and then he starts talking to the birds.)

SAMUEL. All right, all right, don't push. There's plenty for ev-eryone. You there! Leave that little one alone. You're always such a pig. No, no, no. That piece is for her! This piece is for you.

(He digs into his bag and tosses out a piece of bread. At this moment, a fashionably dressed woman, CLARISSA, enters. SAMUEL no-tices her and his posture immediately changes. He seems to close in on himself, as if closing ranks. CLARISSA looks around and then she spots SAMUEL. She freezes. She looks as if she doesn't know whether to stay or go. Finally, she begins to walk toward SAMUEL. When she arrives, she is quite nervous. SAMUEL does not look up at her.)

CLARISSA. *(At last, speaking awkwardly.)* Hello.

(SAMUEL says nothing. He continues throwing crumbs at the birds.)

CLARISSA. Excuse me? *(SAMUEL looks up at her briefly, then goes back to feeding the birds.)* ... You don't... recognize me, do you?

SAMUEL. *(A beat, then gruffly.)* Should I?

CLARISSA. Well, no... I mean, actually, I'm glad you don't. I... well, I was here yesterday, in this park...

SAMUEL. Yeah?

CLARISSA. I'm the one who... took the video?

SAMUEL. *(A beat.)* I don't know what you're talking about.

CLARISSA. *(Very uncomfortable.)* Oh, God, I knew I shouldn't have come. It was probably all my imagination.

SAMUEL. Look, lady. You got something to say? Spit it out or get lost, okay?

CLARISSA. Oh, God. I... don't you remember? I was... walking down this path here and... well I had my video camera on. I was with my husband? And I took your picture.

SAMUEL. *(He's remembering now, with rancor.)* Oh... yes... So that was you.

CLARISSA. Look I didn't mean... ! We're on vacation here... my husband and I, from L.A. and—

SAMUEL. And you don't have enough freaks to take pictures of there?

CLARISSA. No! I mean... I didn't know when I took your picture you were... you had... I thought it was... charming.

SAMUEL. What?

CLARISSA. I'm saying this all wrong! What I mean is I saw you, all bundled up against the Seattle morning air, with hundreds of birds around you. Birds at your feet, on your arms, on your shoulders, it was amazing! Don't you... see? That's what I was taking the picture of... not what you... think. It was only once I put the video on the hotel TV, where everything was in color, and took a closer look, especially during this part where I'd... zoomed in. It was only then that I... *saw*...

SAMUEL. The *real* me?

CLARISSA. *(A beat.)* Yes. And I saw something else, too. You were... looking right at us. At me. Taking that video. And you looked like...

SAMUEL. What?

CLARISSA. Like you wanted to kill me.
SAMUEL. Yes. Well, I probably did.
CLARISSA. So. That's why I'm here.
SAMUEL. So I can kill you?
CLARISSA. No! So I... can... explain!
SAMUEL. Fine. You've explained.

(He looks away from her and tosses more crumbs to the birds. CLARISSA stands there.)

SAMUEL. You can go, now.
CLARISSA. That's... it?
SAMUEL. What did you expect?
CLARISSA. I don't know... I just hoped...
SAMUEL. That I would help you expiate your guilt? No such luck, lady.
CLARISSA. But you have to understand, I never intended—!
SAMUEL. What? To be cruel? Maybe not. But you were. *(A beat.)* Look. Whatever it was you came for, you're not going to get it. So why don't you just go back to your fancy hotel and let me get back to my birds. *(CLARISSA does not leave.)* Go! *(Still, CLARISSA does not budge.)* I said, get lost! *(Although she looks shaky, CLARISSA remains. SAMUEL speaks with bitterness building to vitriolic anger.)* Shit. Do you know what it feels like to have a video camera aimed at your face, lady? At *this* face? It's like being pinned under a fucking microscope. And there's not a thing you can do about it. Other than slamming the camera into whatever perfect little face is taking the picture that day! Kill you? Damn straight I wanted to kill you! And if you don't leave right now, I may still do it! *(He waits for her to leave, she doesn't.)* What the hell are you waiting for?!

(CLARISSA stands there, clearly frightened. But she doesn't move.)

CLARISSA. *(A beat.)* I can't.
SAMUEL. Why not?
CLARISSA. *(Another beat, plaintively.)* I don't know.

(There is a long pause. Finally, SAMUEL starts gathering up his things.)

SAMUEL. All right. Then *I* will.

(He starts to leave.)

CLARISSA. *(Reaching out and touching his arm.)* No! Please!

(SAMUEL swings around to find himself face to face with CLARISSA. He stares her down, daring her to look at him. It is intensely uncomfortable for both of them. CLARISSA does not look away.)

CLARISSA. Please.

(SAMUEL settles back on to the bench. He is silent. There is a long pause between them. Finally SAMUEL speaks.)

SAMUEL. Look, lady...
CLARISSA. Clarissa.
SAMUEL. Clarissa, look. If—
CLARISSA. Would you... consider... *(She digs in her purse.)* ... taking this?

(CLARISSA draws out a camcorder tape from her purse and extends it toward SAMUEL.)

SAMUEL. No.
CLARISSA. Please, uh... Mr.... ?
SAMUEL. *(Begrudgingly.)* Samuel.
CLARISSA. Samuel. Take it. It will be useless to me now.
SAMUEL. What are you talking about? You get to that part, you can tell a chilling little scarface tale.
CLARISSA. I don't want to show this to anyone.
SAMUEL. This is stupid. You have lots of other stuff on this tape, don't you?
CLARISSA. Some things.
SAMUEL. Sight-seeing shit. Memories...

CLARISSA. It's all right.

SAMUEL. I could put it in my VCR. I have one, you know.

CLARISSA. I don't doubt it.

SAMUEL. Invite all my friends over. I have some of those too, you know.

CLARISSA. I'm sure of it.

SAMUEL. And we could watch all your personal shit. We could laugh about you.

CLARISSA. Is that what you would do?

SAMUEL. Maybe.

CLARISSA. Well then, do it.

SAMUEL. Are you crazy?

CLARISSA. I invaded your privacy. You have the right to invade mine.

SAMUEL. So that's what you think this is? A tit for tat?

CLARISSA. No!

SAMUEL. You think this little tape is going to make everything even?

CLARISSA. No, I don't! I just thought you would want to—!

SAMUEL. Keep your goddamn tape. You bleeding hearts are all the same. You think you can put a toe into the sea of suffering, wiggle it about, and say, I'm with you, brother!

CLARISSA. Please... Samuel.

SAMUEL. No.

CLARISSA. Take the tape!

SAMUEL. Unh, unh, I'm not going to make it that easy for you.

CLARISSA. What do you want, then? I'll do it! Just tell me!

SAMUEL. I want you to leave me the hell alone! *(A beat.)* Look, Clarissa, go home. Go back to that two story postmodern you and hubby own in the hills. Go relieve the grandparents of your kid, no, make that *kids*, you wouldn't be the type to let your eldest languish as an only child. Go pick up the life you left as part-time mother, part-time...

CLARISSA. Substitute teacher.

SAMUEL. Substitute teacher. And flush this whole thing from your mind. Because that's where it's going to end up anyway, down the drain with all the other flotsam and jetsam you don't know what to do with because, face it, Clarissa, nothing ever really sad or violent or cruel pierces that well-intentioned, well-insulated life you lead! So why don't you just call this an unfortunate little incident and get the hell out of my space! *(There is a long pause as CLARISSA stares at him. She is close to tears.)* Ah, hell.

CLARISSA. You're right.

SAMUEL. Look, I'm just blowing off.

CLARISSA. No, you're right.

SAMUEL. Hell, lady, I do this, all right? I make categories: You suburban housewife, me freak.

CLARISSA. No. It's more than that. How did you—how could you know?

SAMUEL. I don't. I've just learned to... watch people, that's all. Funny thing happens when people are afraid to look at you. Makes you invisible. There's a hell of a lot of observing you can do when you're invisible.

(CLARISSA grows thoughtful.)

CLARISSA. Yes. *(A beat. She puts the videotape back in her purse.)* I'm sorry I bothered you, Samuel. I shouldn't have come.

(CLARISSA turns to leave.)

SAMUEL. Before you go... *(Surprised, CLARISSA turns around.)* I would like to ask you something.

CLARISSA. Yes?

SAMUEL. Why did you come?

CLARISSA. Why? I told you, I—

SAMUEL. No. I mean, what made you come? Most people they... well, they might *think* about coming. They'd maybe have a few days of guilt, but hell, they wouldn't actually *come*, you see what I mean?

CLARISSA. Yes, I guess I do.

SAMUEL. So what made *you* come?

CLARISSA. Well, I almost didn't. I had to really talk myself into it. I was terrified.

SAMUEL. Yeah, I have that effect on people.

CLARISSA. No, it wasn't that ... All last night, I couldn't sleep. I kept seeing the way you had looked at me, on the video. And then,

was like I was inside it, looking from behind it. And I felt such a
age! I wanted to tear all the sheets apart. And I was the cause of it.
That rage! That's what frightened me. Don't you see? I can't bear
dding to it. To the horribleness of the world. I yell at one of my
hildren and I see his look. And I know I've added to it. I slough off
friend who needs me because I can't stand to hear her complain,
nd I add to it. I buy the wrong product from a company that poisons
s workers in a factory in Mexico, and I add to it! But still, until
esterday, I thought, if only I were more vigilant, if only I tried harder,
could change. But then, I did what I did to you. Without awareness,
ompletely accidentally. And it struck me. It's inescapable! There's
o way not to add to it! Every day. By breathing. By being! I don't
nderstand! I'm not on this earth to hurt people, I can't believe any
f us are. Why is it that's all we seem to do? Do you know? Why?

*he is crying softly. She drops down on the bench next to SAMUEL.
Although he is awkward with this, for the first time he looks at her
with something akin to compassion.)*

SAMUEL. *(Shaking his head.)* Human fucking nature.
CLARISSA. *(Deeply felt.)* I'm so sorry, Samuel.

*LARISSA looks at him. SAMUEL looks back and there is a mo-
ment of real connection between them. This moment is almost too
intense for SAMUEL. He looks away and preoccupies himself with
the bag of bird crumbs. Taking this as a cue, CLARISSA gets up
and begins to walk away.)*

SAMUEL. Maybe... *(CLARISSA turns around.)* It ain't all bad
t there, Clarissa ... Hell, *you* came back, didn't you?

LARISSA smiles. Lights fade to Black.)

THE END

by

JOHN STINSON

MEDIAN
by John Stinson

Directed by **Michael Bigelow Dixon**
Dramaturg **Corby Tushla**

Hays ....Michelle Enfield
Danny ....Mark Burns
Scotty ....Robert G. Cui

Scenic Designer **Stephanie R. Gerckens**
Costume Designer **Kevin R. McLeod**
Lighting Designer **Kathleen Kronauer**
Sound Designer **Martin R. Desjardins**
Properties Designer **Mark Walston**
Stage Manager **Sarah Nicole Spearing**

MEDIAN

(A thin grassy median strip dividing a highway. DANNY, a boy in his 20s, sits on the grass, looking at the cars zooming by. He looks at his watch, then returns his gaze to the road. He looks again, spots something he recognizes, then looks away at a different part of the traffic. A blaring horn is heard, followed by another. HAYS, a woman in her 20s, pitches onto the median, landing near DANNY and puffing hysterically.)

HAYS. What the hell are you doing out here?

DANNY. Waiting.

HAYS. Did you see me almost get mauled.

DANNY. Yeah. First one looked like a Beemer. You'd have gotten a lot of dough.

HAYS. I almost got killed.

DANNY. Then again, they might not give you any money. I think crossing a highway's illegal.

HAYS. I know it is. And I know why. It's incredibly stupid.

DANNY. Well, only you can judge that about yourself.

HAYS. How long have you been out here?

DANNY. Since rush hour. This morning. Eight-forty. I crossed on over to the middleground. Speeds were like this. Fuckin-A-fast.

HAYS. This is, then, a suicide attempt of sorts?

DANNY. Am I dead?

HAYS. Doesn't look it.

DANNY. No suicide. You?

HAYS. Concern for a friend. Not suicide.

DANNY. The way you deal with onrushing traffic, I might not

have known. You gotta pick your lane and keep constant speed. That way the terrified motorists can gauge how best to avoid smashing into you.

HAYS. I didn't quite consider their end in the whole situation.

DANNY. You gotta think beyond your own skin, Hays.

HAYS. Fuck you. And fuck this banter. Hi Danny. What the hell are you doing out here?

DANNY. Waiting.

HAYS. For?

DANNY. Rush hour. So I can go home.

HAYS. You're crossing back over?

DANNY. Yep. I expect twenty minutes from now will be prime time. Though it's packing up pretty good already. What the hell are you doing out here?

HAYS. I've been looking for you all day. Managed to spot you out here. Was stupid enough to run over here since you wouldn't acknowledge my presence on the other side.

DANNY. Thought that was you waving and flapping your arms. But it's so hard to see past all these cars. I really wish they wouldn't put them in our way when we're trying to party.

HAYS. You are being an incredible jerk.

DANNY. Well, you were a moron to come out here. At least I've got a legit reason to be sitting here.

HAYS. And that is?

DANNY. I hate my petty problems. Dodging a roaring Buick makes me forget them. Plus, life's less boring.

HAYS. So this is some thrill-seeking expedition?

DANNY. Sure there's some thrill in it... You know, if I hadn't already made people think I'm a liberal, I'd join some war. That's perfect. I'd like to get in on some of that.

HAYS. I guess it's my job to convince you otherwise?

DANNY. I didn't force you to follow me out here.

HAYS. I came anyway.

DANNY. I know. And I think you should seek professional help. This could be indicative of a larger problem.

HAYS. I care about you.

DANNY. Believe it or not, I feel the same about you. Didn't expect you to go running into that shit, though.

HAYS. Neither did I.

DANNY. So why did you? People who care call the paramedics or Nurse Ratched or something. Why'd you take the leap of doom?

HAYS. You haven't finished telling me why for you.

DANNY. H-A-Y-S.

HAYS. I was worried I might be one of the reasons.

DANNY. Yeah?

HAYS. Yeah.

DANNY. Well, don't worry. It's just that I feel shitty.

HAYS. You don't have to feel that way.

DANNY. What way do you think I feel?

HAYS. If I had to guess?

DANNY. Yeah.

HAYS. Useless. You feel useless. To the universe.

DANNY. That's the problem with having friends, they get to know you inside and out.

HAYS. And that's what I mean. You don't have to feel that way. You've got friends. Friends who love you.

DANNY. Convince me that love will make me not feel this way.

HAYS. It's not that easy. Things take a little more sweat than that.

DANNY. Then I'd rather feel this way.

HAYS. Thanks. Thanks a lot, Danny. You grant me a whole lot of value with that one.

DANNY. I didn't mean it. But you know, we aren't even lovers.

HAYS. I can't love my best friend?

DANNY. Are you sure that's all?

HAYS. Yeah.

DANNY. Sure?

HAYS. Yeah, that's all.

DANNY. *(Getting up, walking toward road.)* Well, then I just better get back across that road. Wouldn't want to be upsetting my friend.

HAYS. Danny.

DANNY. No, no. I'm all right. Friend.

(DANNY steps a little into traffic.)

HAYS. Okay, okay! I like you more than that. You big stupid asshole.

DANNY. Sorry. You sit out on a median all day, Hays, and you start to lose hope for humanity. Watching thousands of mechanized egos in full armor at ramming speed.

HAYS. Yeah, well, all those mechanized egos fly home but when they walk into the apartment or whatever, the answering machine has two blinks going. That's two friends incredibly glad to hear that person's voice when she finally calls. You know? This is not because they're all doing it. It's because we give up those ridiculous egos and just breathe with each other and admit that it's pretty hard sometimes. But we make contact and we live outside ourselves a little.

DANNY. Man. I thought a soundtrack was going to kick in.

HAYS. I'm serious.

DANNY. I know. I'm just being an asshole.

HAYS. So what do you have for me?

DANNY. Okay, I also guess I came out here hoping you'd get mad and give up on me. Then I'd have to chase you for a change. Maybe I'd actually do something.

HAYS. But I followed you, as always.

DANNY. Yeah, you did. Right to the fucking median.

HAYS. The only way to get me to give up on you is to treat me real bad.

DANNY. And I wouldn't treat you bad. Not real bad.

HAYS. You'd just treat you bad.

DANNY. Yeah.

HAYS. And you never see any link between those things?

DANNY. I guess not. (HAYS gets up and walks toward the edge of the highway. She jumps forward into a lane and leaps right back out.) Cut it out! Cut it out!

HAYS. Get it?

DANNY. Yeah. A little. I get it a little.

HAYS. Look at me. Look at me everyday.

(A loud horn is heard, followed by another. SCOTTY pitches onto the ground near DANNY and HAYS.)

SCOTTY. Hey. Hey you guys! Check this out, I made it across, too. Could have been Ford Fodder. Could have been Mack Truck

Meat. Could have been Jeep Juice. But I made it. Oh. Are you guys having a moment? I could just, you know, turn back around... *(SCOTTY faces the traffic again. Turns back around right away.)* No. That would be completely insane.

HAYS. Scott, come sit down over here.

SCOTTY. So what the hell are you doing here?

HAYS. I followed him.

SCOTTY. What the hell's he doing out here?

HAYS. It's as close as he could get to Bosnia.

SCOTTY. Turn on the TV, Danny-boy. You get plenty of Bosnia.

DANNY. Yeah. Well. What are you doing out here?

SCOTTY. Didn't want to miss out.

HAYS. On what?

SCOTTY. On whatever this is. You got to admit, seeing two people running around a median strip at rush hour—it's tempting. There has to be something up with that. So what are you guys doing here?

DANNY. Watching humanity suck.

HAYS. Nothing.

SCOTTY. Really?

HAYS. We were just hanging out.

SCOTTY. Oh. You're just... sitting?

HAYS. More or less.

DANNY. She chased me, Scotty. Couldn't help herself.

HAYS. I couldn't help that you act like this and I have to come hold your hand.

DANNY. Hey, I was doing fine, and would have been home ten minutes from now and you'd have never known.

SCOTTY. You guys want me to migrate down the median a bit?

DANNY. Nah. I was just kidding. I was all mopey and Hays came out to talk to me. It was very sweet of her.

HAYS. Thanks.

SCOTTY. You're surprised by this?

DANNY. I guess not. I guess I shouldn't be. That Hays, she's a real samaritan.

HAYS. You know, I know about your wanting to chase me. That's why I never run. I know it messes with you. I love that. Part of why I let you get away with this stuff.

DANNY. Yeah?

HAYS. Yeah.

(DANNY looks at HAYS for a second, looks again to the road, and leaps up and out to the traffic. HAYS turns her head and the honking blares.)

SCOTTY. Jesus, Dan! Dan! Back in the war zone. *(Pause.)* He made it. Barely.

HAYS. I don't care.

SCOTTY. You want to go after him?

HAYS. No. No, I don't. I won't. *(SCOTTY pulls out a pack of cigarettes and offers one to HAYS. She shakes her head 'no.' He pulls the pack back, then immediately offers it again. HAYS takes the cigarette.)* Thanks.

SCOTTY. Hays? Do you like him?

HAYS. I don't think I get to.

SCOTTY. Yep. You want to stay here? You're sure?

HAYS. Not about much.

SCOTTY. It's safer here.

HAYS. Yeah. It is.

THE END

THE GUEST OF HONOR

by

RICHARD STRAND

THE GUEST OF HONOR
by **Richard Strand**

Directed by **Vladimir Prahcharov**

Karen ....Jan Harlin
Lynn ....Pip Tulou
Jason ....James McDaniel
David ....Eric McNaughton

Scenic Designer **Paul Owen**
Costume Designer **Kevin R. McLeod**
Lighting Designers **Jonathan Bumpas** and **Suzanne Mulder**
Sound Designer **Sean Vail**
Property Master **Mark J. Bissonnette**
Production Stage Manager **Judy Clemens**
Assistant Stage Managers **Megan Wanlass** and **Brad O. Hunner**
Dramaturgs **Tanya Palmer, Matthew Southworth, Michelle Spencer** and **Michele Volansk**

THE GUEST OF HONOR

KAREN. So, what's he like?

LYNN. See, that's the thing about him: he's really no different from, say, you or me.

JASON. Exactly. That's how I feel. He's like, you know, just a person. That's the only thing that matters. Just a person. No different, really, from any other person.

KAREN. How marvelous. A person. Uh, what's wrong with him?

LYNN. Nothing. That's the point. In a very real sense, there is nothing wrong with him.

JASON. Exactly. And that is very well put. There's really nothing wrong with him. That's how we should always look at it.

KAREN. How wonderful. Uh, is there some reason I might *think* there was something wrong with him?

LYNN. No. That's the amazing thing. There is really no reason you would ever think that there is something wrong. Because of his attitude. He's got a great attitude.

JASON. Exactly. We have these prejudices and fears, but they are all unfounded. They are meaningless. And he, maybe more than any man I know, is proof of that.

LYNN. A shining example, really. A shining example of the indomitable nature of the individual.

KAREN. Wow. That's great. Uh, forgive me for seeming a bit thick here, but what prejudice and fears should I have about him?

JASON. None. That's the point.

LYNN. Exactly. For all intents and purposes, he is a man like any other man.

JASON. And that's how he likes to be treated.

KAREN. Yes. Yes. I understand, and, of course, I'm sure you're right. But, you know, if I *were* to have a prejudice or fear about him, what would that prejudice or fear be?

JASON. Karen, the whole point is that you should feel no such thing.

LYNN. Yes. That's the point we're trying to make.

KAREN. Oh, I understand. And I agree with you. Absolutely. Down the line. All the way. Believe me, I'm in your corner. Only, I was sort of hoping that you might give me a clue, you know, of what sort of prejudices and fears I might, if I were less sensitive, be tempted to have so that, you know, I could sort of push those aside as soon as I felt them rearing their ugly little heads. You know.

JASON. Karen, believe me, you will be so comfortable with him that you won't be tempted, even for a second, to think of him as anything other than a person, a human being, one of us, a friend, a colleague, and a wonderful guy.

(The doorbell rings.)

LYNN. That's him. Okay, now, Karen, don't say anything embarrassing.

KAREN. Like what?

LYNN. You know. Just don't say anything that shows you're self-conscious.

JASON. Because, really, there's nothing to be self-conscious about.

LYNN. Exactly. He's just a person. That's really the only important thing. That he's a person.

KAREN. Well, of course. That is the important thing. Only, do you think you could give me an example of something embarrassing I might say so that I could have a solid hold on what I shouldn't say?

LYNN. Say anything you like, Karen. He's a man, that's all. And no different from you or me. Not in any way that matters.

KAREN. That's certainly good news. Only I'd still like one example of a truly embarrassing thing that I might say so that I could avoid saying it.

JASON. You're worrying too much. Relax.

(The doorbell rings again.)

LYNN. I better let him in.

KAREN. NO! Not yet! I'm not ready!

LYNN. Ready. Ready for what? Karen, you're making way too much out of this.

KAREN. *(Grabbing LYNN.)* You can't open the door. Not yet. Not until you give me an example of an embarrassing thing that I might say.

JASON. This is just silly.

KAREN. Tell me. I mean it. Tell me.

JASON. He's at the door. We have to let him in.

KAREN. TELL ME! TELL ME SOMETHING I MIGHT SAY THAT WOULD BE REALLY EMBARRASSING. TELL ME NOW!

LYNN. Jason, can you think of something?

JASON. Well, sure. Uh, let me think...

LYNN. Oh. I know. You know, just as an example, don't say something like, "Master, I found a letter for you at the institute this morning; it was addressed to Arbois."

JASON. Sure. That's a good example.

LYNN. You know, it might make him feel self-conscious.

JASON. Right. Just a little sensitive.

(The doorbell rings again.)

KAREN. Why would I say that?

LYNN. Well, frankly, I can't imagine that you would which is why this whole conversation is so ridiculous.

JASON. I agree. You're becoming obsessed by this. When the whole point is, he's no different from anyone else.

LYNN. Exactly. *(The doorbell rings again.)* I can't continue to leave him out there, Karen. You have to let go of me so I can open the door.

(KAREN lets go. LYNN answers the door and DAVID enters. As advertised, he is, in no important way, different from you or me.)

(In the following dialogue, LYNN, DAVID and JASON all speak simultaneously.)

LYNN. *(Taking a bottle of wine from DAVID.)* David! Thanks for coming and what's this? You brought wine? That's wonderful! Thank you. Thank you so much.

DAVID. *(Giving LYNN a bottle of wine.)* Here. I brought this for you. It's not a real expensive... you know, just a little gift. For you. And Jason.

JASON. Take your coat? Oh, sorry. You're not wearing one. Well, thanks. Thanks a lot.

(Continuing normally.)

LYNN. And David, this is our very good friend, Karen. Karen, this is David.

DAVID. Hi. It's a pleasure to meet you.

(KAREN is conspicuously staring at DAVID, looking for the problem. DAVID becomes quite self-conscious. So do LYNN and JASON. LYNN nudges KAREN.)

KAREN. Oh! Uh, uh, of course... *(KAREN looks to LYNN, very afraid she will say something wrong. Her next words are very stilted. Everyone is staring at KAREN, hanging on each word.)* It's, uh, a-pleasure-to-meet-you-too.

(Everyone heaves a sigh of relief. DAVID is smiling broadly.)

LYNN. Let's sit down.

JASON. I'll get wine glasses.

(JASON exits to get wine glasses. LYNN manipulates KAREN into sitting next to DAVID on the sofa.)

LYNN. So, David, Karen writes shareware.

DAVID. Really!

KAREN. Yes. Yes I do.

DAVID. That's fabulous.

KAREN. It's okay.

DAVID. What is shareware exactly?

KAREN. Well, it's nothing really. It's just software. Only it's marketed differently from software that you might buy at a computer retailer.

DAVID. How so?

KAREN. Well, instead of buying a program for tens, or sometimes hundreds, of dollars, you pay a nominal price and try it out on your computer.

DAVID. I see.

KAREN. Then, if you like it, you send money to the programmer. Usually something like ten or twenty dollars.

DAVID. I see.

KAREN. And, if you don't like it, well, you just delete it from your hard drive and you don't have any further obligation.

DAVID. *(Taken aback.)* I beg your pardon?

(LYNN looks mortified. JASON comes running back into the room to smooth things over.)

(JASON, LYNN and KAREN all speak the following lines simultaneously.)

JASON. I don't think she really meant that you would just delete it from your hard drive...

LYNN. What Karen means...

KAREN. Did I say something?

LYNN. Right. Or that there would really be no further obligation...

JASON. Right. Not in the sense of, you know, an obligation...

KAREN. Oh no. I didn't mean...

(They continue normally.)

LYNN. I think what Karen meant was...

JASON. Karen can speak for herself, dear.

LYNN. Of course. I'm sorry. Karen, why don't you just clarify what you meant.

(All eyes are on KAREN.)

KAREN. I,... uh,... I can't really even remember what it is I said that I didn't mean.

JASON. Well, you *said* that you could delete it from your hard drive...

KAREN. Oh, right. And what I *meant* was, uh, you could, uh... *erase* it from your, uh, *data storage device.*

DAVID. *(Relieved.)* Oh. Oh, I see.

JASON. And, Karen, you also *said* that you wouldn't have any further obligation.

KAREN. Right. Right. I *said* that. But what I *meant* was that you, you know, wouldn't have any *subsequent commitment.*

(Everyone relaxes and feels better.)

DAVID. Oh! Oh! Of course. I see now.

JASON. Subsequent commitment.

LYNN. *(Laughing.)* Makes all the difference, doesn't it?

DAVID. *(Laughing.)* Well, sure. Subsequent commitment.

JASON. *(Laughing.)* She just *said* further obligation. She *meant* subsequent commitment.

KAREN. Right. And all I was really trying to point out is, that the whole thing is on the honor system.

(Everyone abruptly stops laughing. LYNN kicks KAREN's ankle. DAVID is again taken aback.)

DAVID. I beg your pardon?

KAREN. Um, um,...

JASON. Uh, again, I don't think Karen really meant to say, "honor system."

KAREN. Well, no. Of course not. Not, "honor system."

LYNN. No. She meant to say...

JASON. Dear! Let Karen say it.

KAREN. Sure I can say it. I meant, uh, not, "honor system," but, uh... integrity... scheme.

(DAVID is even more taken aback. LYNN kicks KAREN's ankle again.)

DAVID. I beg your pardon?

KAREN. And, really, I didn't even mean, "integrity scheme," as much as I meant, uh,... morality... structure.

(DAVID is even more taken aback. JASON shakes his head in disbelief. LYNN kicks KAREN's ankle again.)

DAVID. I *beg* your *pardon*!?

KAREN. And, actually, I didn't even mean, "morality structure," because what I really meant was, uh, uh, *(She is pretty sure she's going to get it wrong again.)* ... scruple... strategy.

(In a pre-emptive strike, KAREN kicks LYNN's ankle. As anticipated, DAVID is even more taken aback.)

DAVID. Excuse me?!

JASON. I think what Karen means...

KAREN. I CAN SPEAK FOR MYSELF, JASON! *(Everyone is silent, waiting for KAREN to do just that.)* I found a letter for you at the institute this morning; it was addressed to Arbois!

(KAREN makes a grand exit. Everyone else is left shell shocked.)

DAVID. *(After a reflective moment.)* You know, I hate to admit this, but I had that coming.

THE END

TOKEN TO
THE MOON

by

BRIAN CHRISTOPHER WILLIAMS

TOKEN TO THE MOON
by Brian Christopher Williams

TOKEN TO THE MOON was first performed at Actor's Theatre of Louisville in August, 1995. It was directed by **Frank Deal** with the following cast:

Smitty ....Nick Sanzo
Doris Ann.. Lori Duff

PRODUCTION STAFF

Lighting Design **Brian Scott**
Costume Design **Kevin R. McLeod**
Sound Design **Shane Rettig**
Dramaturg **Lesley Tsina**

TOKEN TO THE MOON

(Manhattan subway stop; 2:30 AM.

DORIS ANN is seated on a bench UC. Her eyes are dreamy and distant, focused just slightly above the paperback novel she holds in her hands. We hear the distant rumbling of the subway. SMITTY, gaunt and poorly dressed, enters DL, quietly shuffling, his eyes fixated on the tracks. He glances down the track, looking for a train. Suddenly he looks up, as if hearing a noise, and slowly turns to face Doris Ann who has not noticed him. He watches her for a few quiet moments before he speaks.)

SMITTY. I used to be able to make myself disappear. *(DORIS ANN slowly rouses, as if waking from a distant dream. She finally sees Smitty.)* Like you were doing. I used to go far away, too. *(DORIS ANN turns her attention to her book.)* "Mona quivered as she felt the heat bursting from Rod's loins." *(DORIS ANN quickly stuffs the book in her bag and moves toward the exit.)* "Don't even look at him. Get yourself out to the street where there's safety, Doris Ann."

(Startled, DORIS ANN turns to face him.)

DORIS ANN. Do I know you?
SMITTY. We've never met.
DORIS ANN. No.
SMITTY. How do I know your name?
DORIS ANN. Yes, how?
SMITTY. I can hear you thinking.
DORIS ANN. No, really. How?

247

SMITTY. I can hear you thinking. *(She turns to go.)* "This city's full of lunatics. You should have stayed in Ohio." *(Stunned, DORIS ANN turns to him.)* Please don't be frightened of me. I used to be able to make myself disappear, go away; not anymore. Such a journey you were taking, imaginative, all the way to the moon.

DORIS ANN. You saw that?

SMITTY. Heard it. From the words you said inside your head. You thought joyfully; freedom, power, omnipotence.

DORIS ANN. Yes. I was moving in slow motion.

SMITTY. Slow motion?

DORIS ANN. Very little gravity; I was virtually weightless. Every movement studied, controlled and effortless. Who are you?

SMITTY. You can call me Smitty.

DORIS ANN. You can hear me thinking?

SMITTY. Yes.

DORIS ANN. This is...

DORIS ANN. ... amazing.

SMITTY. *(Simultaneously.)* ... amazing?

(DORIS ANN nods. Smitty shrugs. She reaches for her purse.)

SMITTY. No, I don't want your money. Besides, you only have some change left from the five dollar bill you gave the dime store clerk to pay for that romance in your hands. I know. I heard you. *(Listens.)* No. You can't stop thinking because try as you might your mind is still working, and even if you try to block me out you're still thinking the words "block him out."

(DORIS ANN giggles.)

DORIS ANN. That's wonderful. I guess I didn't have to tell you that. You already knew I was thinking that.

SMITTY. You must be an English teacher.

DORIS ANN. Why?

SMITTY. You think in complete sentences. Most people think only in nouns; train, clock, tile, bench; very dull. Or they think in exclamations; Hey! Ow! Fuck! Oh, pardon me.

DORIS ANN. That's really very interesting.

SMITTY. Is this just the sort of thing you were hoping to find when you left Ohio? *(Listens.)* Oh, does she look just like you?

(DORIS ANN looks almost horrified.)

SMITTY. I can hear the things you don't want me to hear. It's not all that much of a blessing. I hear things I don't want to hear, also. Believe me when I tell you there are a lot more things I don't want to hear than you don't want me to hear. The Midas touch.

DORIS ANN. Pardon?

SMITTY. All King Midas touched he turned to gold. At first glance, it was a blessing, but when he reached out to touch those he loved... life-sized lawn statues. So, he could no longer touch. And when he lost the ability to touch, he also lost the ability to feel. *(Listens.)* Who's Claire?

(DORIS ANN is visibly agitated.)

SMITTY. You know you can control your thoughts. I can only hear what you're actually thinking; not what you're hiding. *(Listens.)* Oh, you're an interpreter, not an English teacher. *(Listens.)* Sixteen languages? My, that's impressive. *(Listens.)* I don't understand. *(Listens.)* No, I don't understand. *(Listens.)* Oh, you can think in another language. Very facile. *(Listens.)* Joy hi him young and june?

DORIS ANN. Joi hni heem chung yao ohn chune.

SMITTY. What language is that?

DORIS ANN. Cantonese.

SMITTY. *(Simultaneously.)* Cantonese.

(DORIS ANN giggles.)

SMITTY. Very clever. What does it mean?

DORIS ANN. In the midst of danger there is safety. It doesn't really translate well into Cantonese.

SMITTY. In the midst of danger there is safety. What made you think of that?

DORIS ANN. I don't know.

(In the distance, we hear the rumbling of the subway.)

SMITTY. What are you doing out at this hour? It's 2:30, you're alone, in a deserted subway in New York. *(Listens.)* No, you're right, it's not deserted if I'm here. *(Listens.)* What? *(Listens.)* What language is that?

DORIS ANN. Finnish.

SMITTY. Finish? I'm just getting started.

(DORIS ANN groans.)

SMITTY. Do you really speak 16 languages? You could work at the U.N.

DORIS ANN. I do.

SMITTY. I swear that one was just a coincidence.

(DORIS ANN giggles.)

SMITTY. Thank you. You have pretty eyes, too.

(DORIS ANN looks away.)

SMITTY. Oh, don't be embarrassed. Sometimes it's actually nice for me to know what somebody else is thinking. *(Listens.)* Alright, I'll change the subject. I'll bet you and your twin had a secret language; that's why you became interested in lang—what wedding? She got married recently?

(DORIS ANN turns to go.)

SMITTY. I'm sorry. Please don't go. I'm begging you. Please!

(DORIS ANN stops.)

SMITTY. I'm sorry. I can't turn it off. I promise I won't talk about her if you can just stop thinking about her. Even if you think about her, I'll try not to notice. Don't go. Please.

(DORIS ANN turns to him.)

SMITTY. I sleep during the day when most people are awake and going about their business. At night, there a fewer voices. It's more manageable. It's quieter down here. Usually it's only me and the track rats. They don't think in English so I don't mind being around them. I guess they have feelings, but I can't hear feelings, I can only hear words.

DORIS ANN. The Midas Touch.

SMITTY. You're singular.

DORIS ANN. I'm what?

SMITTY. Different. Special. No, you are.

(He taps his head.)

SMITTY. Inside. You express yourself so clearly. You'd be surprised how often people don't say what they mean or mean what they say.

DORIS ANN. Have you always been this way?

SMITTY. And you choose to change the subject because... ? *(Listens.)* No, I haven't always been this way. *(He puts his hands up in defense.)* Please. I'd like to tell you, but... *(Pause.)* How long have you been in New York?

DORIS ANN. And you choose to change the subject because... ? *(Pause.)* Six months.

SMITTY. Six months?

DORIS ANN. I wanted to come my entire life, but...

(He hears her thought.)

SMITTY. I'm not noticing. I promise. *(She smiles. He smiles.)* Tell me about the U.N. that must be very interesting work.

DORIS ANN. Not really. I'm just a tool.

SMITTY. Please?

DORIS ANN. No one actually speaks to me. What I mean is when they speak to me they aren't really directing conversation toward me. They aren't soliciting my opinion. Bits of information get fed into two holes in my head. All I do is spit that information out another hole.

SMITTY. But you've changed it. The information went through you, you processed it, you made it comprehensible, and then you gave birth to a whole different beautiful being.

DORIS ANN. But they weren't my words to begin with. I have—

SMITTY. —no original thought.

DORIS ANN. Exactly.

SMITTY. You have an affinity for language the way Betty Crocker knows recipes.

DORIS ANN. But even Betty Crocker has creative control. She gets to decide how much flour, how much spice. She gets to decide whether to bake, sauté or broil. Comparing me to Betty Crocker is like comparing fingerpainting to the Sistine Chapel.

SMITTY. But could Betty Crocker whip up a trip to the moon?

(DORIS ANN smiles.)

SMITTY. I used to daydream all the time. I would go on fantastic journeys. Exploring with Magellan or horseback riding with the Indians or deep-sea diving with Jacques Cousteau. I envy you.

DORIS ANN. It's just a form of escape. Even if you go to the moon you still have to come back to earth.

SMITTY. But you got to go to the moon.

(Beat. We hear the distant rumbling of a subway car.)

SMITTY. You have tremendous control. No more words?

DORIS ANN. I was just looking at you.

SMITTY. No thoughts?

DORIS ANN. You look thin.

SMITTY. I do look thin.

DORIS ANN. Are you ill?

SMITTY. It's difficult for me to eat.

DORIS ANN. If only I had that problem.

SMITTY. With so many distractions, so many stimuli, it's difficult to focus on anything, eating included.

DORIS ANN. What do you do?

SMITTY. Do?

DORIS ANN. Work. Where do you work?

SMITTY. You think I'm a vagrant.

DORIS ANN. No, I don't. I... yes.

SMITTY. I don't work. I can't.

DORIS ANN. You don't really do much of anything.

SMITTY. You're reading my mind?

DORIS ANN. No.

SMITTY. Don't let me make you sad.

DORIS ANN. You don't make me sad.

(Beat.)

SMITTY. I'm trying not to notice.

DORIS ANN. I want you to notice. Go ahead. Notice. What's to hide? I used to be able to do what you do. I could read Claire's mind and she could read mine. You were right. We had a language all our own. We had a world all our own. But it was all in here. *(She taps her forehead hard.)* Our world... my world was all in here. She got married and now it's ended. What do you do when your world has ended?

SMITTY. But—

DORIS ANN. Not but. And. She got married *and* it ended. I've never had anyone else in my life except Claire. My hopes, my dreams, they all breathed because of her. *And* now she's gone and I don't have a life.

SMITTY. You made a new start. You moved to New York *and* you made a new start.

DORIS ANN. I might as well have moved to the moon.

SMITTY. Things could be worse.

DORIS ANN. What the hell does that mean? Things could always be worse. Why do people say that? Is that somehow supposed to be some sort of a consolation? Yes, Grandpa's dead, but at least he died in his sleep; things could be worse. For who? Grandpa? I bet if he could tell it, he'd say things could be a hell of a lot better.

SMITTY. I didn't mean anything by it.

DORIS ANN. I know. I know. Look, I know in the big race I'm not going to win the prize for having the most miserable life that ever happened, but somehow that just doesn't make me feel any better.

SMITTY. I'm sorry.

(SMITTY starts to walk away.)

DORIS ANN. Hey, where are you going? Hey, I'm sorry. Don't go. *(DORIS ANN runs behind him and wraps her arms around him.)* Please don't go.

(He doesn't struggle to get away, but he cannot turn to face her either.)

SMITTY. I used to drive train. This was my line. This was my last stop. There's safety in danger. You said that before. You'll have to explain that one to me. I know there's danger in danger. He was just a high school kid. He was on the tracks on a dare, they tell me. Those moments before, I've played them over and over in my head. I was a daydreamer, you know. I used to go exploring with Magellan and horseback riding with the Indians and... I remember looking at the control panel. I remember calling my stop. "57th Street. 57th Street Station." I loved driving train. I don't remember daydreaming that day. But I have doubts. We don't remember all of our night dreams. Why should we remember all of our daydreams? And I saw him there on the track. At first I thought I was watching a movie or television. Why would someone actually be standing on the track? And he didn't move. And I realized this was real, this was life, he was on the track. He was scared and he couldn't move. And I saw his eyes. And I heard his voice in his mind. He was screaming in his mind like he was trying to wake up from a nightmare, but he couldn't wake up. And I heard his voice in his mind. He said. No. *(She comforts him. She takes his hands and guides him to the bench where she puts his head on her shoulder.)* Go ahead. Tell me things could be worse. I deserve that.
DORIS ANN. No. Things couldn't be worse. Isn't that comforting?
SMITTY. Not really.
DORIS ANN. But they will get better. Someday.
SMITTY. Someday.

(Beat.)

DORIS ANN. Hey, you want to go someplace?

SMITTY. I'm very vulnerable right now. Are you trying to seduce me?

DORIS ANN. Yes. *(He turns to her.)* I know a place we can go where there's very little gravity.

(She leans back against the wall and shuts her eyes. He takes her hand, leans back against the wall and shuts his eyes. The rumbling of a distant subway car can be heard as the lights fade to Blackout.)

THE END

CONTRACT WITH JACKIE

by

JIMMY BRESLIN

CONTRACT WITH JACKIE
by Jimmy Breslin

CONTRACT WITH JACKIE was first performed at the 1996 Humana Festival of New American Plays, March, 1996. It was directed by **Frazier W. Marsh** with the following cast:

Jackie ....Divina Marsh
Newt.. William McNulty

Scenic Designer **Paul Owen**
Costume Designer **Kevin R. McLeod**
Lighting Designer **T.J. Gerckens**
Sound Designer **Martin R. Desjardins**
Properties Manager **Ron Riall**
Stage Manager **Lori M. Doyle**
Dramaturg **Michael Bigelow Dixon**
New York Casting Arrangements **Laura Richin Casting**

CHARACTERS
JACKIE
NEWT

PLACE
A hospital room in Atlanta, 1980.

CONTRACT WITH JACKIE

(Hospital room, Emory University Hospital, Atlanta, 1980. Woman in bed with post-op IV's. Husband enters.)

NEWT. I'm here—1980's most promising freshman congressman and the groundswell that's gonna produce the third wave information age post-industrial society. How are you, Jackie?

JACKIE. I didn't think you felt anything about me anymore. You never even call.

NEWT. I'd have to lose the sight of God not to come here.

JACKIE. *(Pleased sound.)* Mmmmmm.

NEWT. You have no idea of the trouble I had getting here from Washington. They actually bumped Newt Gingrich off a Delta flight. How can they do that to me? They said they were overbooked. They can't make room for a United States Congressman flying home to his own district in 1980. I noticed two flight attendants getting on. I said what about them, why can't they wait for the next flight. The ticket counter person said, "Oh, they're needed in Atlanta." I was never so insulted in my life. I am going to have the FAA close the Delta Airline rest rooms. *(JACKIE makes sound of pain.)* Do the doctors know if they got it all this time?

JACKIE. They seem to think so. But that's what they thought when they operated on me the first time.

(Pause.)

NEWT. *(Smiling as he looks into briefcase and brings out a yellow legal pad. He draws a line right down the middle. From here on, he makes notes as he talks.)* How's the house? You know I haven't really looked at it for a whole year.

JACKIE. The bookshelves in the den look like they're going to just fall down. The washing machine makes a noise like a truck. The garage door won't go up. I sure could use you. I guess I let things go too long.

NEWT. With all due respect, that's why I really think it's a spectacularly good idea for us to spend some time together right now. We have a lot to talk about, Jackie. I have a general vision of where I want this marriage to go.

(He makes a note on the pad.)

JACKIE. We're going on a good seven months with this separation.

NEWT. The girls call and tell me about you, but sometimes I'm going so fast in Washington that I'm not able to listen carefully. *(Closes eyes and smiles.)* NEWT! NEWT! NEWT! It's a weird experience. I don't like it at all. What with being alone, separated form the daughters, too. But we have to have the... moral courage to change or perish. I want to come out of here today with some very positive changes.

JACKIE. You've done pretty well. You got through colleges and to Congress. Who knows better than me? I paid for all your degrees. The one graduate school loan, I paid most of that off, too.

NEWT. *(Writing furiously.)* Jackie, when I get power someday, that's the first thing I'm going to go after. That loan could have made me a pauper. That loan represents a sick, helpless society. These limp-wristed yellow draft dodgers who get a Ph.D. so they don't have to hear a gun fire. Higher education is out of control. The anti-Vietnam radicals dominate the faculties. They teach destruction of our culture. We're subsidizing cowardice and petty barbarism.

JACKIE. You didn't go to Vietnam, either.

NEWT. I had two daughters. It would have made no sense to go into the army just because there was a war. Besides, colleges should give people the commitment to solve real problems. If you're homeless, then just get a home and then you're not homeless. If you're unemployed, get a job and now you're employed. If you need food, go to the store. If you're a weak yellow coward liberal, then get some backbone and you won't be a cheap draft dodger. You can be a war hero.

JACKIE. Newt.

NEWT. What?

JACKIE. I'm glad you're here. I missed you. Do you think we might have a chance?

NEWT. Of course we have a chance. We can change our lives and change society, too. Not to be egotistical, but I'm the same honorable, moral man I was when you married me. But I can see more now. I can see things in the context of the whole society. Listen. Learn. Help. Lead. NEWT! NEWT! NEWT! NEWT! I also know what compassion truly is.

JACKIE. I could use some of it this time.

NEWT. But the more important thing, I'll tell you the great example, I made a positive speech on the floor that affects you and this entire country. Jackie, in the third wave information age post-industrial society, you are going to sit in your diagnostic chair at home, sensors will take your blood pressure, analyze a blood sample, do throat cultures. You only go to a hospital when something is seriously wrong. If you have some life-threatening disease, information systems will allow you to study the most advanced work all over the world. Jackie, this hold by this medical guild has been broken. It's just an opening to a new beginning in medicine. And I thought of you when I spoke about it.

JACKIE. Newt, these computers don't work in cars. How do I sit in a chair and find a tumor?

NEWT. Jackie, that's the sheer brilliance of the idea. If anyone in this country needs a specialist, a databank at your fingertips gives you a range of choices, based on cost, reputation and outcome patterns.

JACKIE. In other words, you don't find the tumor.

NEWT. Yes, but the doctors who specialize in tumors are in the databank at your fingertips.

JACKIE. By the time the databank gets the doctor's name, he's either retired or dead. So am I, by the way.

NEWT. But remember that we're only at the new beginning.

JACKIE. A man with an aneurysm was in one of the operating rooms yesterday. They said he had the worst headache of his life, and that was the only symptom. The symptom after that is known as bingo.

NEWT. In the third wave information age post-industrial society, we're going to find out about these things simply by tapping the right key.

JACKIE. *(Grunts.)* If you have an aneurysm, do you just put your head back in the chair and wait for it to explode?

NEWT. That's just a detail. I know there will be advances that will help you. Just let me say one thing. You mention cars. You still have the Volkswagon, right? *(She nods and he makes note.)* And I have the Thunderbird.

JACKIE. You got it at cost when they told the assembly plant manager that you were going to win the elec—What are you writing down all the time?

NEWT. Show it all to you in a minute. First, I want this one thing straight. There is nothing illegal if the assembly plant at Hapeville sells me one of its cars at cost right off the assembly line. *(JACKIE has a pain spasm.)* All right?

JACKIE. Uh huh. Look at me. I thought I'd be in New York this week looking at Impressionists.

NEWT. New York! What do you want to go there for?

JACKIE. I went to all that trouble saving my money every week for a trip to New York and look where I wind up. I wanted to see the Impressionists at the Metropolitan Museum.

NEWT. How could you even consider going there with your money? You can't bring anything to New York. The federal government sends billions to New York and the Mafia steals it all. You have the Mafia there because of these cheap liberal wimps.

JACKIE. Does the Mafia have that much of a hold on New York?

NEWT. Second only to Israel. All the fault of the liberals. Just like the French. The Germans came through Caen on the Belgian border in 1871, then in 1914. These limp liberal French disarmed. In 1940, the Germans poured through Caen again. It's precisely the same thing in New York. *(JACKIE shows pain or discomfort.)* I understand this kind of pain and suffering and anguish. We've been through this once before. Cancer is a test of the soul, of our resolve to triumph over a deadly foe and go on to a better, more prosperous, rewarding, enriching life.

JACKIE. Newt, that's a campaign speech.

NEWT. With all due respect, I really mean what I'm saying.

JACKIE. Newt, I was standing right next to you while you made this same speech in Monticello. At the Farmers Market. About my first operation.

NEWT. I only introduced you that night.

JACKIE. You told them right out loud, "The cancer my wife has just been through. Please vote for us."

NEWT. I may have mentioned you were ill.

JACKIE. Deathly ill was your phrase.

NEWT. If I did bring it up, it was only to appeal to the sense of faith and religion of the audience. Certainly, I wasn't using it for votes. Only somebody shallow and despicable would use his wife's cancer to get ahead. Besides we were right in the furnace of a political campaign.

JACKIE. Sometimes it was fun to be in a campaign.

NEWT. You always told me you hated them.

JACKIE. I didn't like it when you told people they had to be nasty.

NEWT. You can't fight fair against these liberal traitors and you've got to be nasty when you fight the lying liberal media. But I didn't think you liked any of the campaigns at all.

JACKIE. Newt, how could I enjoy most of them? I had my teaching job. I had two little girls at home. And I had cancer. But you know what I was thinking of? Making all those peanut butter and jelly sandwiches.

NEWT. When that Shapard has a Democrat barbecue, fifty dollars a head, I just knew what we had to do. Get up a mountain of peanut butter and jelly sandwiches and give 'em away free.

JACKIE. I started making them the night before and never stopped.

NEWT. They charged fifty dollars for listening to nothing. That's the Democrats for you. But we gave the people free peanut butter and jelly to show I was one of the common folks. And then they listened to my new, great ideas. We have to teach more about Benjamin Franklin. Make drug users pay up to a third of their gross assets. Let's see some cocaine snorting shortstop pay a million dollar fine. And I was the first to point out that there are literally hundreds of babies left in dumpsters in Washington, D.C. You can't fit a newspaper in because of all the dead babies stuffed in the dumpster. That's the fault of our liberal national elite and their insane welfare policies.

I told the people my stunning, unique and totally brilliant idea on how to end welfare. We will take all the women and children off welfare and there will be no more welfare. *(He claps hands together.)* Lord, isn't it wonderful to be able to see ahead! Remember when I told them that, Jackie? How there wasn't a sound in the crowd when I talked?

JACKIE. They had their mouths stuck together with peanut butter.

NEWT. That peanut butter and jelly was the best idea I had. It was forward thinking. The best.

JACKIE. I thought I was the one thought of the peanut butter and jelly.

NEWT. Then that Democrat woman Shapard handed it to us when she said that if she got elected she wouldn't make her family move to Washington.

(He smiles broadly.)

JACKIE. Yeah, you made me write a letter to all of the garden clubs saying that she was going to break up a family unit, and that we were going to go to Washington together. Remember I wrote, "Let our family represent your family in Congress." I wasn't so proud of that.

NEWT. I was. I said her family values were the same that cause these welfare people to be out killing, murdering, and slaughtering people in the cities. And I let good decent people know how we lived as a family in Carrolton, Georgia.

JACKIE. And they all had a pool going on election night as to how long we'd last together in Washington.

NEWT. That was all those Democrats. They're all sick, vicious enemies of mine. Limp liberals.

JACKIE. Newt, your own press secretary won the pool. Dave Worley. He bet on a breakup inside of eleven months. He sure was right.

NEWT. No, that old fat liberal, Shapard, was at the bottom of that.

JACKIE. I wish you wouldn't call her that. I'm slightly overweight myself.

NEWT. Ole fat liberal.

JACKIE. *(After pause.)* Was that what happened with me in Washington? I got too heavy?

NEWT. Uh, naw, well, so much went on.

JACKIE. Was it my age? Newt, I'm the same seven years older that I always was. When you started coming onto me in the back of my geometry classroom. I could hardly believe it. I was the teacher and I got a high school kid looking at me. And me liking it! What did I do, suddenly seem older in Washington? With all those young wives? Do you think that you can't be the Speaker or get to the White House with a wife looks like me?

NEWT. *(Looks up from writing on pad.)* Jackie, with all due respect, I didn't come here to hurt you. Believe me, I'm the same compassionate man I always was.

JACKIE. And you know I wouldn't do anything to turn the girls against you.

NEWT. Oh, I know that. If there is one thing I know about you it's that you're loyal. Loyalty. I want to thank you for having it, Jack—

JACKIE. —I don't know so much if it's loyalty. That sounds like a political word. It's just I was raised in Columbus, Georgia, to be a lady and never diminish the reputation of the father. Even if he isn't worth the effort.

NEWT. *(Jumps up impulsively.)* And you're still a lady from Columbus.

JACKIE. *(Struggles to sit up and smiles faintly.)* Come here.

NEWT. *(Energetically going to bedside and instead of kissing her, thrusts pad in front of her.)* Here.

JACKIE. What is this?

NEWT. Why don't you just sign it. That'll give us an agreement.

JACKIE. What kind of agreement?

NEWT. A divorce.

JACKIE. A wha...? What are you talking about?

NEWT. A sensible settlement. And speedy. You'll never see me in a negotiation that breaks down.

JACKIE. Newt, I cant' sign anything without a lawyer.

NEWT. A lawyer! We've allowed lawyers to run our affairs. Who are they? Scurrilous people who get rapists and child molesters off. We ought to remember that. Every time you hire a lawyer, you help a rapist.

JACKIE. I didn't expect this from you.

NEWT. Jackie, do you realize how sick that is? Have you lost all your family values? Do you realize how truly sick you are?

JACKIE. That's what the doctors say.

NEWT. I can't stand here and see you like this... If it's too much for you to read, here: "Newt. Clothing allowance, four hundred a month. Jackie, alimony, nothing." Let me explain the alimony. If I get three suits and you have no new clothes, then just by me having three new suits, you will have a new outfit. That's the American dynamic. But if I pay alimony to you... in other words if you go on welfare... you'll be weak and dependent on handouts. You can cure people on welfare. Every time they moan, tell them to go out and open a business. They have to learn a hard lesson in self-reliance Just like you, Jackie. *(With this, she puts her head back on the pillows and falls asleep.)* If it's too much for you to sign, just initial it.

(Lights fade to black.)

THE END

25 Ten-Minute Plays
from
Actors Theatre of Louisville

Foreword by Jon Jory

SPADES by Jim Beaver

BREAD by Andy Backer

ATTACK OF THE MORAL FUZZIES by Nancy Beverly

EATING OUT by Marcia Dixey

APRES OPERA by Michael Bigelow Dixon and Valerie Smith

THE ROAD TO RUIN by Richard Dresser

THE DRUMMER by Athol Fugard

PERFECT by Mary Gallagher

LOYALTIES by Michael Guyer

"THE ASSHOLE MURDER CASE" by Stuart Hample

DOWNTOWN by Jeffrey Hatcher

ELECTRIC ROSES by David Howard

4 A.M. by Bob Krakower

AMERICAN SAINT by Adam LeFevre

WATERMELON BOATS by Wendy MacLaughlin

INTERMISSION by Daniel Meltzer

LOVE AND PEACE, MARY JO by James Nicholson

MARRIED BLISS by Mark O'Donnell

SUBTERRANEAN HOMESICK BLUES AGAIN
by Dennis Reardon

THE FIELD by Robert Spera

COVER by Jeffrey Sweet
with Stephen Johnson and Sandra Hastie

THE DUCK POND by Ara Watson

LOOKING GOOD by John W. Williams

COLD WATER by Lee Blessing

CAMERAS by Jon Jory

More Ten-Minute Plays
from
Actors Theatre of Louisville

Edited by Michael Bigelow Dixon
Foreword by Jon Jory

Ten-Minute Plays
from
Actors Theatre of Louisville
Volume 3

Edited by Michael Bigelow Dixon and Michele Volansky
Foreword by Jon Jory

Ten-Minute Plays
from
Actors Theatre of Louisville
Volume 5

Edited by Michael Bigelow Dixon and Michele Volansky
Foreword by Jon Jory

More Popular Plays

by

JANE MARTIN

CEMENTVILLE

CRIMINAL HEARTS

JACK AND JILL

KEELY AND DU

MIDDLE-AGED WHITE GUYS

TALKING WITH …
A Collection of Monologues

VITAL SIGNS
A Collection of Monologues

WHAT MAMA DON'T KNOW
A Collection of One-Act Plays:
Cul-de-Sac
Shasta Rue
Travellin' Show
The Boy Who Ate the Moon
Summer

Other Publications for Your Interest

CINDERELLA WALTZ
(ALL GROUPS—COMEDY)
By DON NIGRO

4 men, 5 women—1 set

Rosey Snow is trapped in a fairy tale world that is by turns funny and a little frightening, with her stepsisters Goneril and Regan, her demented stepmother, her lecherous father, a bewildered Prince, a fairy godmother who sings salty old sailor songs, a troll and a possibly homicidal village idiot. A play which investigates the archetypal origins of the world's most popular fairy tale and the tension between the more familiar and charming Perrault version and the darker, more ancient and disturbing tale recorded by the brothers Grimm. Grotesque farce and romantic fantasy blend in a fairy tale for adults.

(#5208)

ROBIN HOOD
(LITTLE THEATRE—COMEDY)
By DON NIGRO

14 men, 8 women—(more if desired.) Unit set.

In a land where the rich get richer, the poor are starving, and Prince John wants to cut down Sherwood Forest to put up an arms manufactory, a slaughterhouse and a tennis court for the well to do, this bawdy epic unites elements of wild farce and ancient popular mythologies with an environmentalist assault on the arrogance of wealth and power in the face of poverty and hunger. Amid feeble and insane jesters, a demonic snake oil salesman, a corrupt and lascivious court, a singer of eerie ballads, a gluttonous lusty friar and a world of vivid and grotesque characters out of a Brueghel painting, Maid Marian loses her clothes and her illusions among the poor and Robin tries to avoid murder and elude the Dark Monk of the Wood who is Death and also perhaps something more.

(#20075)